GEARÓID ÓG
NINTH EARL OF KILDARE

Historical Association of Ireland
Life and Times Series, No. 12

Gearóid Óg
Ninth Earl of Kildare

MARY ANN LYONS

Published for the
HISTORICAL ASSOCIATION OF IRELAND
By Dundalgan Press Ltd

First published 1998
ISBN 0-85221-135-X

To
Enda

© Mary Ann Lyons 1998
Cover design: Jarlath Hayes
Cover illustration: Portrait of the ninth Earl of Kildare, 1530,
sometimes attributed to Holbein
Historical Association of Ireland, Dublin
Printed by Dundalgan Press, Dundalk

FOREWORD

This series of short biographical studies published by the Historical Association of Ireland is designed to place the lives of leading historical figures against the background of new research on the problems and conditions of their times. These studies should be particularly helpful to students preparing for Leaving Certificate, G.C.E. Advanced Level and undergraduate history examinations, while also appealing to the general public.

CIARAN BRADY
EUGENE J. DOYLE
Historical Association of Ireland

PREFACE

The sixteenth-century portrayal of the demise of the Kildare dynasty in 1534 left to us by Richard Stanihurst, a close friend of the eleventh Earl of Kildare, is one which has coloured interpretations of the events surrounding the family's destruction for generations. The present study of Gerald Fitzgerald, or Gearóid Óg as he has been more familiarly known to generations of history students, sheds light on the career of a man who has for too long been cast in the shadow of his more charismatic father and his more colourful son. The career of Gerald, the ninth earl, merits individual study given that his political capabilities, his role in the fall of the house of Kildare, and the political circumstances leading to the removal of the Kildares have undergone fundamental reappraisal in recent years thanks to the scholarship of Steven Ellis in particular and also that of Brendan Bradshaw, D. B. Quinn and Laurence McCorristine. This book is therefore a synthetic work which draws together literature, both old and new, concerning the Fitzgerald dynasty and specifically Gerald and the political milieu within which he operated in the late medieval/early modern period.

A number of people have assisted me in the completion of this work. My thanks to Colm Lennon for reading a draft of the text and for his encouragement, to Steven Ellis for his advice regarding the portrayal of the ninth earl, and to Eugene J. Doyle for his editorial work. Finally, I owe a special word of thanks to Ciaran Brady and Colm Croker for their painstaking editing of the text.

MARY ANN LYONS
College of Humanities
University of Limerick

CONTENTS

CHRONOLOGY 1

INTRODUCTION 5

1. The Inheritance and Succession of Gerald,
   Ninth Earl of Kildare 9

2. Continuity and Rumblings of Reform, 1513–19 . . 22

3. Kildare–Ormond Rivalry, Thomas Cromwell and
   the Weakening of Geraldine Autonomy, 1520–33 . . 33

4. Cromwellian Reform and the Geraldine Revolt
   of 1534 51

CONCLUSION 68

NOTES 70

SELECT BIBLIOGRAPHY 75

CHRONOLOGY OF GERALD FITZGERALD'S LIFE AND TIMES

1487	Birth of Gerald Fitzgerald. May: Lambert Simnel, pretender, crowned king in Christ Church, Dublin.
1495	Eighth Earl of Kildare and his son Gerald at the English court.
1496	Eighth earl returns to Ireland; pact agreed between the earl and Henry VIII; Gerald detained at the English court as surety for the earl's continued loyalty.
1503	Aug.: Gerald marries his first wife, Elizabeth Zouche, in England and returns to Ireland.
1504	Feb.: Gerald is appointed Treasurer in the Dublin administration. Aug.: battle of Knockdoe in Galway.
1508	Gerald in England.
1509	Apr.: death of Henry VII; accession of Henry VIII.
1513	Sept.: death of the eighth earl; succession of Gerald as ninth Earl of Kildare. Nov.: Kildare appointed Lord Deputy. Birth of Thomas, his son, in London.
1515	May–Sept.: Kildare at English court to answer complaints regarding his governorship. Aug.: death of seventh Earl of Ormond; succession dispute between the earl's daughters and his cousin, Sir Piers Roe Butler of Polestown. Henry VIII authorises several favours for Kildare, very probably including an act conferring liberty status on County Kildare.
1516	Piers Roe recognised as Earl of Ormond.
1517	Death of Gerald's wife at Lucan, County Dublin.
1518	Commencment of the 'Kildare Rental Book'; Kildare seeks licence to establish a college at Maynooth.
1519	Kildare summoned to court (departs *c.* Oct.).
1520	Mar.: Thomas Howard, Earl of Surrey, appointed Lord Lieutenant (arrives in May). May: Kildare bound to remain in the London area. June: accompanies Henry to the Field of the Cloth of Gold in France. Nov.: released on sureties. Marries his second wife, Lady Elizabeth Grey.

1

1521	Sept.: Surrey requests his own recall (departs for London in Dec.).
1522	Mar.: Piers Roe Butler sworn as deputy. June: Desmond intrigues with envoys of Francis I.
1523	Jan.: Earl of Kildare returns to Ireland. Feb.: asserts his privilege to nominate the candidate to be appointed to the see of Kildare. May: campaigns in Ulster. Dec.: James, Gerald's brother, murders Robert Talbot of Belgard while he is *en route* to spend Christmas with Ormond in Kilkenny.
1524	May: Kildare reappointed Lord Deputy; Ormond appointed Treasurer. June: commission to resolve feud between Kildare and Ormond. July: indenture between the two earls on levying coign and livery.
1525	Kildare, the council and commissioners in Dublin fail to reconcile Conn Bacach O'Neill and Aodh Dubh O'Donnell.
1526	Aug.: Thomas Dillon, Henry VIII's candidate, provided by the papacy to the see of Kildare. Dec.: having appointed his brother, Sir Thomas Fitzgerald of Leixlip, as his deputy, Kildare departs for England to answer charges levied against him by Ormond.
1527	Kildare examined before the king's council; not convicted. Sir Thomas Fitzgerald resigns. Sept.: Richard Nugent, Lord Delvin, appointed deputy to Kildare. Dec.: Desmond campaigns in Ormond's territory.
1528	Feb.: Piers Roe Butler created Earl of Ossory. May: Delvin captured by O'Connor Faly at Kildare's instigation. Aug.: Ossory appointed Lord Deputy.
1529	Feb.: Bishop Walter Wellesley of Kildare signs his name to a list of opponents of Kildare. Aug.: 'secret council' of three officials, Rawson, Alen and Bermingham, appointed deputy to Henry Fitzroy, Duke of Richmond and Somerset (titular Lord Lieutenant). Aug.: arrival of royal commissioner, Sir William Skeffington. Sept.: provision of John Alen as Archbishop of Dublin.
1530	June: Skeffington appointed Lord Deputy. July: Kildare is one of several temporal and spiritual lords who sign a petition to Pope Clement VII asking him to accede to

Henry VIII's petition for divorce. Aug.: Skeffington and Kildare return to Ireland; both attack O'More of Leix. Gerald's portrait painted by Hans Holbein.

1531 Feb.: Henry VIII recognised as 'Supreme Head of the Church of England' by convocation of Canterbury. Sept.: Skeffington's parliament.

1532 Jan.: third session of 'Reformation parliament' at Westminster. July: Kildare attends court and is appointed Lord Deputy; Ossory appointed Treasurer; Archbishop George Cromer appointed Chancellor to replace Archbishop John Alen.

1532 Thomas Cromwell, Henry VIII's secretary, assumes supervision of Irish affairs. *c.* Dec.: Kildare sustains a gunshot wound during the siege of Birr Castle.

1533 Jan.: Henry VIII marries Anne Boleyn. Feb.: fifth session of 'Reformation parliament' at Westminster. June–July: Charles V's envoys in Ireland to negotiate with Desmond. July: Clement VII excommunicates Henry VIII. Aug.: Kildare receives an official reprimand from Henry VIII. Sept.: Kildare begins transferring the king's ordnance to his own strongholds. *c.* Sept.: Kildare, Ossory and other officials summoned to court.

1534 Jan.–Mar.: sixth session of 'Reformation parliament' at Westminster—break with Rome completed. Feb.: Kildare departs for England, having appointed his son, Thomas, Lord Offaly, as his deputy. Mar.: arrives in London; the earl is known to be terminally ill and begins sending home his personal retainers; examined by the English council and found culpable of several offences; Ossory enters into an agreement with Henry VIII to acquiesce to the Cromwellian reforms. May: Lord Dacre in the western marches of England is arrested on charge of treason. June: Offaly resigns and renounces his allegiance to Henry VIII; Kildare arrested and imprisoned in the Tower of London. July: Archbishop John Alen assassinated by Geraldine supporters; Skeffington appointed Lord Deputy. 2 Sept.: Gerald dies in the Tower. Aug.–Oct.: Earl Thomas besieges Dublin. Oct.: Skeffington arrives with relief army. Dec.: Lord Dacre granted a royal pardon.

	c. 18 Dec.: parliament at Westminster attaints the ninth and tenth Earls of Kildare and their supporters
1535	Mar.: Skeffington besieges and captures Maynooth Castle. Geraldine envoys visit Rome (May) and Spain (June) to solicit aid. Aug.: Thomas surrenders and is taken to the court in England by Lord Leonard Grey where he is imprisoned (Oct.).
1536	Feb.: Grey appointed Lord Deputy; arrest and transfer to England of Earl Thomas's five uncles. May: Irish 'Reformation parliament' convenes in Dublin—act for the attainder of Gerald, ninth Earl of Kildare, and Reformation legislation. July: act for the attainder of Thomas, tenth Earl of Kildare, and his five uncles.
1537	Feb.: Thomas, Earl of Kildare, and his five uncles executed at Tyburn, London.

INTRODUCTION

Gerald Fitzgerald, ninth Earl of Kildare, is undoubtedly better known as Garret Óge or Gearóid Óg as he is usually called in Gaelic annals. However, the use of the Gaelic form of his name is somewhat misleading, since Gerald was an Anglo-Irish magnate. Recognition by Gaelic annalists of his fundamentally Anglo-Irish identity is best exemplified in the Annals of Connacht, which refer to him as Gerald. In terms of historical treatment, the ninth Earl of Kildare has had the misfortune to be identified as the son of the Great Earl of Kildare, Garret Mór, traditionally associated with the establishment of the Kildare dynasty, and as the father of Silken Thomas, the impetuous youth held accountable ever since Stanihurst for the dynasty's demise. His end, according to Stanihurst, was especially tragic: he had been so profoundly affected by Thomas's revolt that 'upon the report thereof he deceased in the Tower, wishing on his deathbed, that either he had died before he had heard of the rebellion, or that his brainless boy had never lived to raise the like commotion'.[1]

The first phase of Gerald's career bore remarkable signs of resemblance to and continuity with that of his father: both remained on amicable terms with the king; both wielded substantial control over the Dublin council; both encountered difficulties arising from internal succession contests in the Ormond lordship; both campaigned to subjugate Gaelic septs and to quell resistance and disturbances in Gaelic lordships. It is hardly surprising, therefore, that more traditional historians have tended to make invidious comparisons between the eighth and ninth Earls of Kildare, almost invariably to the latter's disadvantage. The ninth earl is deemed to have been less successful in fulfilling the joint roles of greatest lord in Ireland and the king's representative than his father had been. He is portrayed as showing no signs of his father's shrewdness or charisma.[2] He was, in short, 'a talented man, partly anglicised . . . he lacked the charismatic quality of his father and never showed himself capable of rising triumphantly above the great challenges confronting him'.[3]

5

Traditional interpretations of the final two years of Kildare rule have been particularly critical of the earl's political ability. These accounts emphasise Gerald's being in such a weakened state that he was incapable of maintaining order in the lordship. His enemies on the Irish council were thought to have conspired against his son, Thomas, tricking the young man into believing his father had been executed and thus provoking him into rebellion. Kildare's removal has been seen as the ultimate outcome of a steady erosion of his power over the previous decade and a half.[4] Ostensibly this rather harsh assessment of Gerald's character and career might seem justified. It was during his time that the coveted deputyship which his father had held for most of his career was assigned to the Kildares' rivals, the Ormonds, as well as to English officials of 'mean birth' such as Sir William Skeffington. It was he who chose to appoint his son, Thomas, as his deputy early in 1534, and it was he who incited his son to rise up in a rebellion against Henry VIII which ultimately brought about the destruction of the house of Kildare.

However, Gerald Fitzgerald is undoubtedly one of the figures in sixteenth-century Ireland who has benefited most from the wave of recent scholarship which has given rise to a fundamentally altered assessment of his life and times. Research in the period, particularly that of Steven Ellis, has exposed the oversimplification inherent in that traditional assessment of the eighth and ninth earls. By setting both men's careers within the broader context of the evolving, modernising Tudor state from the 1480s to the mid-1530s, one can identify fundamental differences between the circumstances obtaining both in the lordship itself and in this wider context during the era of the eighth earl and that of his son. Only recently has there been due recognition of the fact that from the early 1520s until his death in 1534 the ninth earl, unlike his father, had to contend with a serious political rival in the person of the Earl of Ormond. In contrast to the findings of earlier studies, he is now being credited for his relative success in managing to maintain his influence as late as 1534. Equally significant is the often overlooked fact that Henry VII, unlike his son, was more pragmatic in the sense of being more readily prepared to forgive Kildare's indiscretions and to acknowledge the limitations which weighed heavily on the English administration in the lordship. Thus the comparisons formerly made have been unduly harsh. Moreover, there has been a tendency on the part of some historians to distort their analyses of relations between Henry VIII and Gerald, stemming from a fixation with tracing in those relations evidence of the origins of the rebellion of 1534.[5] Yet, as this study will show, those assessments have made little allowance for the fact that Gerald had virtually no control over many of the overarching political changes which were afoot in the Tudor state at that time.

In the era of the eighth earl royal government depended not so much on a developed centralised bureaucracy but rather on the monarch's personal relations with the nobility and gentry of his dominion, with aristocratic delegation being viewed as a pragmatic means of providing reasonably stable government in the lordship. By contrast, the ninth earl of Kildare's career, like those of Lord Dacre and Lord Percy in the northern marches of England, coincided with a change in the character of royal government and policy with respect to both outlying areas of the realm and also to the international situation. This change was particularly marked from the early 1530s onwards when Thomas Cromwell's reform programme for the government of England and Ireland exhibited a new drive to integrate the outlying areas of the realm, including Ireland, more fully into the king's sovereign state.[6]

The ninth Earl of Kildare's career thus spanned a critical period of transition during which he and his father had evolved from being medieval lords administering a medieval lordship to being opponents of a mounting tide of challenges to the dynasty's position of authority and influence in the Dublin administration. This biography therefore will recount his persistent and skilful efforts to retain his prominent position in the Dublin administration which was becoming increasingly modern and bureaucratic, particularly from the early 1530s. Far from being the hapless father of the foolhardy Thomas, Gerald Fitzgerald emerges as the orchestrator of the revolt of 1534. His mistake was not, as Stanihurst would have it, that he had appointed an immature youth as his deputy, but rather that he had misjudged the king's particular sensitivity to and intolerance of any show of resistance in the realm owing to the delicacy of the international situation in the mid-1530s. This, combined with his misguided belief that he could induce Henry to recognise his indispensability to the government of the lordship, as he had managed to do so often in the past, and his concomitant refusal to countenance any reform which involved even a slight diminution of his power, ultimately resulted in the downfall of his family and the dissipation of his political inheritance.

1

THE INHERITANCE AND SUCCESSION OF GERALD, NINTH EARL OF KILDARE

In August 1513, while engaged in a routine campaign against the O'Carrolls of Offaly and besieging their castle at Lemyvannan, Gerald Fitzgerald, the eighth Earl of Kildare, was shot by one of the O'Mores of Leix. Severely debilitated by his injuries, he died on 3 September at the age of fifty-six.[1]

A man who had survived several political mistakes and some broken periods of service as royal governor, Garret Mór had attained the standing of the greatest Anglo-Irish magnate to emerge from the lordship during the fifteenth century.[2] To succeed such a man was not going to be an easy undertaking. His heir, Gerald, was born to his first wife, Alison FitzEustace, in 1487; he was referred to as 'Garrett McAlison' by Gaelic annalists (the latter arising from recognition of Alison's reputation as a great patron of Irish poets).[3] His birth coincided with the most serious crisis in his father's relations with Henry VII. In May 1487 the eighth earl crowned Lambert Simnel, a Yorkist pretender to the English throne, as 'King Edward VI' in Christ Church Cathedral in Dublin and summoned a parliament to confirm 'Edward VI's' claim to the crown of England. The Simnel adventure was an unmitigated failure; yet by the time the ninth earl succeeded to his inheritance in 1513 the house of Kildare had not only recovered from the disaster but had established an unprecedented autonomy in its relations with the English crown.

The Kildare ascendancy was not inevitable: it was, in fact, of quite recent origin. Although they ranked first among the great Anglo-Irish dynasties who had been invested with land in return for service rendered during the Norman invasion in the twelfth century, and although the head of the family had enjoyed the status of earldom since John Fitzgerald had been created first Earl of Kildare in 1316, the careers of successive earls in the later middle ages provided no hint of the heights which their successors were to attain in the late fifteenth century and the early decades of the sixteenth century.[4] The origin of the Kildares' remarkable rise may be traced to the 1450s, when civil war in England caused English involvement in Ireland to sink to its lowest ebb, and to Thomas Fitzmaurice's succession as the seventh earl in 1456 and his subsequent appointment as deputy, a position he held intermittently until his death in 1478.[5] Once they had secured this position of prominence, the Kildares were loath to revert to their former status as the most senior comital family in Ireland or to relinquish their grip on the deputyship; and remarkably, in the half-century that followed, a combination of factors worked to enable them to sustain that ambition.

One crucial determinant of their establishing a virtual monopoly on the deputyship in the period 1470 to 1515 was the absence of any real rival for that office in the lordship. During the early fifteenth century one of the crown's favoured families had been the Butlers, Earls of Ormond, whose base was Kilkenny Castle and whose lands extended across Counties Kilkenny, Tipperary and Waterford. However, the power of that dynasty had been eclipsed with the death of the 'White Earl' in 1452, and his successor took up residence in England, where he became involved in supporting the Lancastrian side in the Wars of the Roses, which ultimately resulted in his execution by order of Edward IV. His brother, Thomas Butler (1477–1515), succeeded him as earl, but continued to live in England, entrusting the dynasty's Irish lands to the custody of cadet branches, the most important of which were the Butlers of Polestown. After the death of Sir James Butler, head of the Polestown branch in 1487, his son, Piers Roe hoped to assume control of the Butler inheritance in Ireland. However, Thomas, the absentee earl of Ormond, appointed James Ormond (Black James), the illegitimate son of his brother, to preside over Ormond property. At this point an Ormond–Kildare feud commenced when Kildare incurred the wrath of Black James by lending his support to the legitimate claimant to the Ormond succession, Piers Roe Butler. However, Kildare's problem with the Ormonds was effectively resolved when Piers murdered Black James in 1497 and the absentee earl resolved to manage his Irish properties through agents while remaining on amicable terms with Piers Roe.[6] The predicament of the Ormonds thus left the way open for the Kildares to monopolise the key post in the administration of the lordship. It was not until Piers Roe, eighth Earl of Ormond (1516) and subsequently Earl of Ossory (1528), emerged as a contestant for the governorship in the early 1520s that the Butlers were seriously to challenge Geraldine authority in the political arena in Ireland. Just how fortunate the eighth Earl of Kildare was to have very little real competition from the Ormonds became apparent during his son's career when this renewed assertion of Ormond power presented a serious impediment to the ninth earl in his attempts to emulate his father's style of government.

The other great Anglo-Irish dynasty, the Fitzgeralds of Desmond, were also in eclipse, having failed in their governance of the lordship during their terms as deputies in the earlier decades of the fifteenth century. The execution of the eighth Earl of Desmond by Edward IV's deputy, Sir John Tiptoft, in 1468 signalled the end of the Desmonds' claim to supremacy, but Tiptoft's immediate failure to establish effective royal control in Ireland, and Edward's appointment of Thomas, seventh Earl of Kildare, as deputy in 1470, established the foundation of Kildare control under royal government.

Their strategic location on the western border of the English Pale was a fundamental advantage that gave the Kildares a powerful edge over their peers in the contest for the deputyship. Since Ormond's attainder in 1462 the epicentre of political influence in the lordship gradually shifted to the Pale, and thus successful government was viewed as increasingly dependent upon cognisance of Palesmen's interests. However, in the period 1470-72 the Dublin administration over which Thomas, the seventh earl, presided was in an extremely vulnerable situation. Sustained attacks by Gaelic septs resulted in widespread disturbances in the Pale and in its greater hinterland, with Counties Meath and Dublin being particularly badly affected. In response to that crisis, and with Edward IV's support, the Dublin council resolved to concentrate upon constructing a defensive system for the Pale which would be less of a drain on the English subvention payment made to the Dublin administration to provide for the upkeep of the defences and government of the colony. In the circumstances, that was as much as they could realistically hope to achieve.

While the early Tudor monarchs' ultimate objective was the extension of royal authority throughout the entire lordship, the continuing lack of the requisite resources and Henry VII's preoccupation with domestic crises ensured that, like their predecessors, their most immediate concern was also provision of adequate defence for the English Pale. Although it is clear that the degree of shrinkage of the Pale in the sixteenth century has been greatly exaggerated, it is nonetheless true that Gaelic raids persisted. Consequently defence remained a primary concern.[7]

Owing to the strategic position of their vast estate, comprising large tracts of land in Counties Kildare, Carlow, Dublin, Meath, Westmeath, Leix, Offaly, Kilkenny, Tipperary and Limerick and with its central point at Maynooth Castle and manor, the Kildares were uniquely capable of providing effective defence of the colony's inhabitants at minimal cost to the royal exchequer. Both successive English governors and lesser Anglo-Irish families (notably the Butlers of Ormond and the Fitzgeralds of Desmond, whose locus lay well beyond the Pale) were unable to forestall raids by neighbouring Gaelic septs, particularly the O'Connors, the O'Mores, the O'Tooles, the O'Byrnes, the MacMurroughs and others. Their impotence stood in sharp contrast with the service rendered by the Earls of Kildare and only served to underscore the latters' apparent indispensability for effective government of the lordship. But the Kildares' strategic position could also be put to effective use in their pursuit of dynastic interests, on occasions at the expense of those of the Pale's community and administration. Both the eighth and ninth earls frequently made shows of their indispensability by capitalising on their strategic position either to mount raids themselves or to incite neighbouring Gaelic septs to attack the Pale with a view towards overawing the government administrators.

By virtue of their strategic location, therefore, the Kildares managed to stake out a greatly extended territory in which both Geraldine and royal authority were at once effectively enforced. It was during the lifetime of the ninth earl's father in particular that the family's manors, centred on Maynooth and Leixlip in northeast Kildare, and indeed the county more generally were transformed from their former vulnerable position to being encircled by a chain of strongly fortified outposts. Arising from his first marriage to Alison FitzEustace, the eighth earl secured a jointure of estates in the south-east and east of the county which bordered on the west Wicklow territory of the O'Tooles.[8] By the 1480s the earl had completed his father's programme of consolidating Geraldine control in Kildare's marches and beginning its extension into other border regions of the Pale. Gradually the incursions made by Gaelic clans into peripheral areas of the county were effectively rolled back: to the south, in County Carlow, Leighlin Castle was repossessed by the eighth earl, and Geraldine castles were also maintained in the county at Rathvilly and Clonmore.

By 1483 encroaching Gaelic septs had been banished from many areas of south Kildare and north Carlow, and the eighth earl immediately moved to secure possession by act of parliament of all waste lands between Calverstown and Leighlinbridge as forfeited property of Irish rebels. Before 1485 he had embarked upon the construction of a castle at Castledermot with a view to reasserting a strategic Geraldine presence in the greater south Kildare and north Carlow region. By the following year that area had been rendered so peaceful that the earl was able to convene a parliamentary session there for the first time in a century.[9] In the south-east marches of Dublin the earl recovered Castlekevin and Fassaroe, and by 1500 he had built Powerscourt Castle.[10] On the western front, by 1500 the O'Connors had been forced to retreat westwards into their heartland in Offaly, Rathangan had been reclaimed, and the earl had managed to repossess the strategically important castles and manors of Lea and Moret. In the north-western extreme of the county the traditionally recalcitrant Berminghams of Carbury aquiesced to recognise Geraldine control, and in 1519 the ninth earl's justices were even to be found administering English law from Carbury Castle. The eighth earl further corroded the advances made by Leinster clans by buying old titles to land and then ejecting the Gaelic occupants. Indeed, soon after his father's death in 1513 the ninth earl had established his authority so effectively as to have secured virtual liberty status for County Kildare. After he appears to have been empowered to appoint judicial and other local government officials independently of the Dublin administration, and certain judicial cases could be heard and rulings delivered in county court sessions without recourse to the king's courts. Another resource which the Kildares harnessed to their dynasty's advantage was the substantial military force which they had at their disposal. As an emergency response, the Kildares had sufficient local forces to mount punitive assaults in retaliation for raids on the Pale. In an effort to address the problem in the longer term, however, the earls resorted to imposing exactions and introducing agreements binding these neighbouring septs to pay tributes to them in an attempt to dissuade the 'wild Irishry' from orchestrating further raids.[11] The seventh, eighth and ninth earls each deployed their own troops to bolster the otherwise inadequate and meagre army and supplies for which the English subsidy made provision. At the battle of Knockdoe outside Galway in 1504, when Kildare inflicted a resounding defeat on the Clanrickard Burkes, the earl fielded an army comprising private retinues and professional soldiers in the pay of himself and others, as well as militias mustered in the English areas of the lordship.[12] The Kildares' military strength was boosted by their creation of a 'set of compacts, enveloping twenty-four Gaelic lords of greater and lesser status in a wide arc about the Pale and farther afield'.[13] Their power as deputies in the Dublin administration was further increased after 1488 when they gained a virtual monopoly on the use of artillery in the lordship, their deployment of siege artillery enabling them to take opponents' fortresses more readily. Kildare's readiness to deploy his private military force and supplies in the service of the king thus proved an irresistably attractive and highly pragmatic solution to the early Tudor monarchs' problem of endeavouring to provide adequate defence for the colony while incurring minimal cost to the royal exchequer.

As deputy, Kildare received rents, fees from judicial proceedings and profits from trade, as well as reaping handsome returns from a range of fees, duties, customs and tithes, in addition to various dues paid either in kind or in service, for example carting days (providing carriage of victuals at a military hosting).[14] Moreover, his incumbency of the deputyship could be exploited for the purpose of augmenting the returns to be derived from his patrimony. This was most explicitly recognised in the terms of the agreement drawn up between Henry VII and the eighth earl in 1496, whereby Kildare was granted the privilege of receiving all crown lands which he could recover from the Gaelic Irish. Furthermore, there is evidence to suggest that while acting as deputy, the eighth earl was taking over the greater proportion of the royal revenues without allowing them to be recorded in the exchequer.[15] Henry VII's officials in the Dublin administration knew that the upkeep of the defence and government of the Pale could either be undertaken by the king at enormous cost or by Kildare at no cost to the royal exchequer. It is hardly surprising, therefore, to find Henry VII being only too glad to revert to dependence on a nobleman who was voluntarily prepared to assume this dubious honour.

Another key source of the Kildare ascendancy was the Geraldines' adherence to the so-called *slánuigheacht* or 'slantyaght' system. In north Connacht and Leinster, Gaelic lords, including MacDermott, O'Rourke, MacRannall, O'Farrell, MacMahon and O'Reilly, were all bound to the Kildares by bonds wherein the earls guaranteed their protection to lesser lords who rendered tributes which were paid in money or in kind and/or military service.[16] In the midlands the chiefs of the most important lordships, namely O'Connor, O'More, MacGeoghegan, O'Dempsey and MacGillapatrick, all adhered to this system, as did their counterparts O'Toole, O'Ryan, O'Byrne, O'Nolan and MacMurrough in south Leinster and O'Dwyer in north Munster.[17] In the case of certain chieftaincies, such as those of MacGeoghegan in the central midlands and O'Farrell and O'Reilly in the north midlands, Kildare asserted his overlordship by buying up pledge lands. Others still, such as MacMahon in south-east Ulster, were kept to heel by having Kildare's galloglas billeted upon their tenants.[18] The earl's 'rental book', commenced in 1518, contains a section entitled 'The Earl of Kildare's Duties upon Irishmen' wherein the names of a total of twenty-four chieftains upon whom Kildare imposed exactions are recorded. These resided in a wide arc surrounding the Pale, and some isolated chieftaincies, such as those of MacDermott and O'Rourke in north-east Connacht and O'Dwyer in north Tipperary, were also listed, testifying to the expansive sphere of

Gerald's influence. In this way successive earls of Kildare managed to construct a network of alliances throughout the lordship which was not based upon traditional territorial divisions, and in doing so they mirrored a strategy which was being adopted by both their English and Anglo-Irish contemporaries.[19] The earls ensured compliance with this system of protection by imposing penalties on those lords who were found to be in breach of the terms of their agreement. Stiff fines of up to sixty or seventy cows or even complete confiscation of the transgressor's territory ensured the continuance of this system, with the latter threat being explicitly recorded as a proviso in the bond between both parties.[20]

At once overlords and royal representatives, the Earls of Kildare, thus stood at the nexus of Gaelic society and the English colony. The paradoxes and ambiguities which shrouded their position, particularly that of the eighth earl, contributed to their success in both roles and to their advancement of both interests, and the two earls manipulated that ambiguity to the full. The accounts of the battle of Knockdoe testify to the manner in which the eighth earl's position was interpreted in many different ways by Anglo-Irish and Gaelic contemporaries. Both the eighth and ninth earls' careers are punctuated with phases when they enjoyed the support of the Palesmen and the monarch while simultaneously wielding immense influence over Gaelic septs throughout the lordship. Until 1515 the Palesmen appear to have accepted the dual character of Geraldine autonomy, no doubt because the eighth earl in particular had been shrewd in ensuring that all campaigns were presented as being undertaken in the furtherance of royal and therefore colonists' interests.

Both earls' careers also feature incidents when they were suspected of connivance with Gaelic allies to the detriment of royal interests. For example, during a campaign led by the Lord Deputy, Sir Edward Poynings, in Ulster in 1494, the eighth earl's negotiations with the Gaelic lords, urging them to submit to the deputy, were viewed by Poynings as treasonable communications and resulted in Kildare's arrest. Yet two years later Henry VII reappointed Kildare as deputy, the latter having convinced him that Poynings had misconstrued his conduct during the Ulster campaign. As Lords Deputy, the earls presided over the administration of royal justice; yet the ninth earl was accused by his opponents in the Dublin council of adopting 'two laws, our prince's laws and brehon laws, which he thought most beneficial as the case did require', as well as allegedly admitting Gaelic customs and fines for felonies similar to Irish law.[21] His alleged practice of coign and livery (a system of uncertain exactions imposed on colonists to support his military retinues) also left him open to accusations of partiality towards Gaelic customs.[22]

In addition, in their private domestic sphere the earls were noted patrons of Gaelic bards and *seanchaidhthe* or 'shanachies', and Gaelic men of learning frequented their castles and those of the collateral branches of the Fitzgerald family throughout the county in the early sixteenth century. Their library at Maynooth Castle contained twenty books written in Gaelic, most of which were devotional works, though the collection also included Gaelic chronicles of Ireland and a work by the twelfth-century Welsh chronicler Giraldus Cambrensis.[23] The ninth earl leased land in Dublin to Gaelic 'rhymers' and retained 'rhymers' and harpers among his entourage.[24] Further evidence of the ninth earl's deference to Gaelic culture is provided in a number of agreements contracted with his Gaelic vassals which were drafted in Gaelic.[25] In 1530, for instance, Gerald enlisted the services of Maoilín Óg, *ollamh* of Síol Muireadhaigh in Abbeyderg, County Longford, who drew up a contract between the earl and MacRannall.[26] Such cross-cultural associations were, however, increasingly regarded by his critics in the Dublin council as incongruous with his position as the king's first representative in the lordship.

The Kildares' insistence upon the pragmatic imperative dictating their recourse to such Gaelic customs and practices served to explain away or at least to mitigate many suspicions of Geraldine partiality to Gaelic ways. Most importantly, while the Kildares dealt with the Gaelic lords through adherence to their own laws and customs, they retained their English identity and their loyalty to the crown. In essence, therefore, the Kildares adapted as best they could to the realities of coexistence between Gaelic and English cultures, exploiting a Gaelic order which they knew they could not overthrow for the advancement of both crown and dynastic interests, while using their position as royal representatives to legitimate that advancement in the eyes of the king, his council in Ireland, the Palesmen, the Anglo-Irish and the Gaelic Irish throughout the island.[27]

As was the case with all aristocratic families, the Fitzgeralds' arrangement of propitious marital alliances also proved an essential strategy in the furtherance of their dynastic interests and expansion of their properties throughout the lordship. Marriages with aristocratic English families, such as that of the eighth earl and his second wife, Elizabeth St John, Henry VII's cousin, in 1496, served to strengthen the relationship of mutual trust between the Kildares and the king. The eighth earl's dynastic strategy is thus reflected in his choice of partners, his first wife having been an Anglo-Irish woman whereas his second wife was English-born. He fathered fourteen children, two of whom died young and one of whom became a Knight of Rhodes. All his remaining children married into English, Anglo-Irish and Gaelic families throughout the provinces, and this served to strengthen the diplomatic network which acted as a fundamental basis for the Kildare ascendancy. Several advantages accrued from such astute arrangements. Firstly, the eighth earl used a marital alliance between his daughter Margaret and Piers Roe Butler, the future Earl of Ormond, in 1505 to achieve one of his most impressive diplomatic coups, the reconciliation of Kildare and Ormond interests. Secondly, through marital associations with leading noble families of the Pale, including the Flemings (Lords Slane), the Darcys of Platten, the Marwards of Meath (Barons of Skreen), the Cusacks of Lismullen, County Meath, the Plunketts (Lords Dunsany) and the FitzEustaces (Lords Portlester), the Fitzgeralds consolidated their cohort of supporters in the Dublin council and administration. Marriage connections with Gaelic families also served to provide an important entrée for the Geraldines into the complex and otherwise impregnable world of Gaelic politics and dynastic interests. Kildare's concern with Ulster is particularly significant: his sister Eleanor and his daughter Alice were married to senior members of the O'Neill clan of Dungannon, and this attachment was to provide the Geraldines with invaluable leverage in Ulster politics, as is evidenced by the influence which they exerted in the history of the succession of the Dungannon O'Neills throughout the sixteenth century.[28] The Fitzgeralds also had close familial associations with the great rivals of the O'Neills in Ulster, the O'Donnells of Tyrconnell. The ninth earl's son Henry was fostered by Hugh Roe O'Donnell (1461–1505), and relations were further consolidated by the marriage between Gerald's sister Eleanor and Manus O'Donnell in 1538. Indeed, several of the Fitzgeralds married twice, and in so doing further enhanced the tapestry of their dynastic alliances. Spurred on by consciousness of his obligation to defend the English Pale from attack by marauding neighbouring Gaelic septs, the eighth earl shrewdly arranged for the marriage of two of his daughters into the O'Connor and O'Carroll clans. Such alliances were undoubtedly also conceived with a view to reinforcing the Kildares' ability to intimidate the Pale with the threat of possible raids.

These were the axes upon which the Kildares capitalised in their ascent to the position of the lordship's premier magnates by the later decades of the fifteenth century. However, their securing the highest political office in the English administration in Dublin resulted from vitally fortuitous external factors which peculiarly worked in their favour. The vicissitudes of the Lancastrian and Yorkist factions in England directly impacted on the balance of power between their respective supporters in Ireland, and the political turmoil in England during and after the Wars of the Roses necessarily served to enhance the standing of the Kildares and the other Anglo-Irish families in the lordship. Like other magnates, the eighth earl of Kildare in the early stages benefited from Henry VII's preoccupation with domestic crises. However, on occasions when he overstepped the mark with the king, most notably in the two pretender incidents (1487 and 1491), Gerald received sharp if short-lived reprimands when Henry intervened directly to ensure the protection of his interests in the lordship.

From their relationship lasting over twenty years, one fundamental lesson was learned by both parties—the fact that, regardless of Fitzgerald's unrivalled position as a leading Anglo-Irish nobleman, his strategic position, his extensive network of dynastic connections, his great military reserves and ammunition, his mastery over Gaelic factions and his enormous personal wealth, the king always had the ultimate power to undermine the most essential axis on which his ascendancy rested by depriving him of the deputyship. By 1496 the two men had arrived at an understanding, and the agreement signed that year set the amicable tenor of their relations for the remainder of the reign. Thus, until his death in 1509, Henry VII regarded the eighth Earl of Kildare as a vital agent in the governance of the lordship and was convinced that commissioning a reliable local nobleman, provided he was adequately supervised, was the most suitable means of government. In the early years of Henry VIII's reign (1509–13) that outlook remained unchallenged and relations remained limited and cordial.

Aged twenty-six, upon the death of his father Gerald was already a man of some experience. Detained at court between the ages of six and sixteen as a surety for his father's good behaviour, Gerald had embraced many of the trappings of court life which set him apart from his father. The flair for fashion so often associated with Gerald's son, Silken Thomas, is in fact attributable to his father, who, even at the age of eleven years, was bedecked in the best of court finery. In 1502, at the age of fifteen, he played the principal role in the funeral ceremony for Henry VII's eldest son, Arthur, in Worcester Cathedral. He received a decidedly English education, gaining exposure to the classics and to the new vernacular Renaissance literature. He also acquired a valuable insight into the machinations of court politics and diplomacy. Most significantly of all, however, his sojourn at court brought him into direct personal contact with officials of Henry VII and, even more important, with young men who were later to become members of Henry VIII's government. Throughout his life Kildare maintained contact with many of the courtiers with whom he had grown up, sending them gifts as tokens of their continued friendship.[29]

His marriage early in 1503 to Elizabeth, daughter of Sir John Zouche of Codnor in Derbyshire, a cousin of Henry VII, confirmed these close connections. The couple were granted lands in both England and Ireland by the king and by the Earl of Kildare, and upon his return home Gerald was promptly appointed Treasurer in the Dublin administration on 28 February 1504, a position he continued to occupy until 1513.[30] Once back in Ireland, he soon gained experience in local politics, though the ineptitude he displayed at Knockdoe was a source of embarrassment.[31] However, after a faltering start, the young

Geraldine heir soon learned the martial skills and tactics which were so essential to the maintenance of his dynasty's ascendant position.

On 4 September 1513, immediately after his father's death, Gerald was elected justiciar by the Dublin council, and two months later, on 26 November, he was appointed deputy by Henry VIII on similar terms to his father's appointment three years previously. The ease with which he succeeded his father seemed to belie any threat. Indeed, continuity with his father's approach to government was to be the most striking feature of the ninth earl's early years as deputy and overlord.

2

CONTINUITY AND RUMBLINGS OF REFORM, 1513-19

The lordship which Gerald inherited in 1513 was already immensely wealthy, and during his time as earl he worked steadily to consolidate and develop its power. Like his father, Gerald used his wealth and his position to project an impressive image of his dynasty's aristocratic majesty. Upon their return to Ireland, he and his wife Elizabeth, their young son Thomas (Silken Thomas) and their four daughters resided at Maynooth Castle. When Elizabeth died unexpectedly at Lucan on 6 October 1517, Gerald was said to have been greatly distressed, but in 1520 he married Lady Elizabeth Grey, daughter of Thomas, Marquis of Dorset. Following their marriage, Elizabeth came to live at Maynooth, and she and Gerald, now in his early thirties, had two sons and three daughters. The elder son, Gerald, the future eleventh earl, was known as the 'Wizard Earl' owing to his interest in alchemy. His younger brother was Edward. The eldest girl, Lady Margaret, was born deaf and mute. Her younger sister, Lady Elizabeth, was acclaimed by contemporaries for her beauty and is reputedly the 'Fair Geraldine' of the famous contemporary portrait. The youngest daughter was Lady Cecily.

The earl enjoyed an annual income well in excess of £2,000 Irish, and he therefore ranked among the top ten Tudor nobility in terms of income, surpassing all other noblemen in the lordship.[1] His household and lifestyle clearly reflected that status.[2] The Kildare households at Maynooth, Kilkea and Portlester were lavishly furnished and had long since borne signs of immense wealth, and the vast collection of silver and gold plate held in each castle was the heirloom of generations of Geraldines.

Corroborative evidence of his enormous wealth and his furtherance of his English humanist education lies in his extensive and remarkably modern library housed at Maynooth in the 1520s. The collection comprised at least thirty-four Latin texts, including the New Testament, the Bible and Giraldus Cambrensis's *Topography*. Thirty-five French texts, including the

Chronicles of France, an abbreviation of the Bible and the story of Lancelot, were also recorded, as were twenty Gaelic texts and twenty-two English books. Some of the material deposited in the library undoubtedly predated Gerald's career, notably his father's certificate of the Order of the Garter which he had received from Henry VII in 1505 on his elevation to the Order.[3] However, the ninth earl's contribution is very evident in his collection of classical works such as *The Destruction of Troy*, *Charlemagne* and a work by the Italian scholar Lorenzo Valla. A number of recent publications added by Gerald, notably the Latin version of More's *Utopia*, *Sir Thomas Moore his book agaynis the new opinions that hold agayns pilgremages* and *The king of Englond his answre to Lutter*, all testify to his interest in contemporary humanist models for social reform and in the early stages of debate in the Reformation controversy.[4] His residence was lavishly decorated and furnished; and Gerald had a portrait executed by the renowned painter Hans Holbein in 1530, and at least one portrait of the earl survived the destruction of Maynooth Castle during the revolt.[5]

In good humanist fashion, Gerald was acclaimed as 'the greatest improver of his lands' in the entire lordship.[6] The 'Kildare rental', commenced in 1518 and containing all details of contracts, terms of leases, tributes, duties, fees, etc. pertaining to his property, testifies to the thoroughness and efficiency with which he administered his estate. It also records details of his improvements in agricultural practices and demesne farming on his estates. He ensured the fiscal well-being of his holdings by obliging every group of three cottagers to supply a labourer for up to one week each year 'to cast ditches and fastnes upon the borders', 'to cut passages upon the borders of Irishmen' and 'to carry stones to the castles on the borders'. Furthermore, if any of his manors were found to be lacking an outhouse, hall, kitchen, barn or stable, the earl's tenants were bound to 'bring the stuff to hand' at their own cost, and Kildare supplied the masons and carpenters for its construction. These repair operations were co-ordinated from the four castles at Rathangan, Maynooth, Athy and Portlester, and in 1518 their supervision on that basis appears to have been a relatively recent development. Apart from rent payments, the earl exacted labour services on many of his manors. Some tenants were obliged to render him '1 turfday, 1 weeding day et 2 hokdays in autumn'. Others owed him three ploughing days for the sowing of wheat and three more for the sowing of oats, along with three days carting turf and three days carting grain. The normal labour service was six or seven days annually, and many tenants were also obliged to present a hen at Christmas time.[7]

The extent of the earls' sway over County Kildare, while very considerable, has in the past been exaggerated by superficial understanding of what precisely the county's liberty status entailed. The privileges granted by Henry to the ninth earl in respect of the towns of Kildare and Athy in 1515 provide an insight into Kildare's liberty. The towns were empowered to have pleas heard in courts presided over by the town sovereign and portreeves (the latter being permitted to act as justices of the peace) and to fill the offices of eschetor, clerk of the market and coroner. Moreover, they were invested with authority to control return of court writs, so that the king's sheriff was effectively excluded from their legal proceedings, and they were also allowed to levy customs and to spend these on town walls and pavements. It is probable that Gerald also received a grant of a similar franchise incorporating the whole of County Kildare at this time. The text of the bill tabled for the granting of such a liberty shows how extensive Kildare's rights and privileges were to be concerning

> all . . . castles, lordships, [manors], lands, tenements, rents, services, [meadows], pastures . . . forests . . . parks, ponds . . . knights' fees, mills, liberties, [franchises], customs, usages, and other commodities, advowsons [rights to nominate clerics to benefices], patronages of abbeys, priories, churches, [vicarages], chapels, chantries [endowments for deceased relatives], prebends [clerical positions affiliated to cathedrals], hospitals, and other benefices ecclesiastical and presentations of the same and all other hereditaments [as once were held by Maurice Fitzgerald, Earl of Kildare].[8]

There is evidence to prove that the liberty of the county, which had originally been granted in the 1290s but which had been suppressed in 1345, was already effectively revived and in operation before 1515. Consequently, Gerald is likely to have regarded the grant of liberty status as amounting to no more than a royal confirmation of Kildare's existing rights.

Yet Gerald's powers, while very extensive, were by no means unlimited. He was not empowered to exercise judgement in the case of pleas of the crown. Thus if anyone in Kildare was found to have committed 'any treason, murder, homicide, rape or any other felony within the said land', Gerald was obliged to convey him to the king's jail, where he was 'to suffer according to the king's laws'. On this basis, the liberty of Kildare fell short of palatine status. Royal commissioners checked on Kildare's adherence to the confines on his authority in order to ensure that he was not engaged in any judicial or punitive activities 'not being determinable within the said liberty'. Controversy surrounded the issue of which officers Kildare was allowed to appoint, and whether and which writs should be issued in Henry VIII's name; and there were objections to the earl's alleged abuse of the liberty through his admission of Gaelic customs and fines as punishment for felonies in a similar manner to brehon law. In 1533–4 Kildare was accused of permitting all pleas, including crown pleas, to be heard before his seneschal. It was also alleged that the earl granted pardons of felonies under his own seal and that he appointed sheriffs and other officers in the county.[9] While Kildare dominated county society, having the power to appoint local administrative and judicial personnel, his supervision of the defence of the county was carried out in conjunction with the county gentry, whose consent and support he could not take for granted. It is likely that the earl had to deal with approximately twenty substantial gentry families in Kildare, most notably the FitzEustaces, the Wogans, the Aylmers, the Suttons, the Berminghams and lesser branches of the Fitzgerald family, who dominated central Kildare, the north-east and the west of the county. It was also from their ranks that he drew candidates to fill local administrative and judicial offices, and his distribution of horses as gifts among these families is evidence of his awareness of his need to court their support. While borough development was encouraged by the earl, in general the county's towns failed to prosper during the Kildare ascendancy, and this has been attributed to the restrictive influence of the earls, who creamed off any profits made, and also to poor agricultural surpluses in the county markets.[10]

In addition to wielding extensive control over the temporal affairs of the lordship, and specifically those of the shire of Kildare, the earls also practised extensive ecclesiastical patronage. As governors of the lordship, the earls enjoyed receipt of restitutions of episcopal temporalities without being obliged to account for those monies. They also retained the right to nominate clerics to livings within the archdiocese of Dublin and the dioceses of Kildare, Limerick, Cork, Meath and King's County as well as to several monastic houses. In addition, the ninth earl received tithe and farm payments from monastic properties in the greater Pale area, as well as rent collected from property which he leased to clerics in English-occupied districts of the lordship. He also received fees from clerics throughout the lordship and within Kildare itself. As in the case of their lay peers, these clerics apparently paid fees to secure the earl's protection against attacks. The ninth earl's influence in ecclesiastical affairs was exerted energetically. He intervened in the appointment procedures of Kildare's monastic houses and the running of priories, including Connell Abbey. His family also had close ties with Grey Abbey in Kildare town and Grey Abbey in Kilcullen, both being burial places of his ancestors, and it was to the White Friars of Kildare town that Silken Thomas, Gerald's son, entrusted some of the family's plate in the wake of the 1534 rebellion. His munificence is evidenced by the fact that a whole host of archbishops, bishops, abbots, priors and deans of Kildare and elsewhere are listed as recipients of gifts of horses from him.[11]

Gerald's foundation of the College of the Blessed Virgin Mary at Maynooth in 1518 was certainly the grandest project in church patronage to have been undertaken by a lay person at that time, and it testifies to the vigour of pre-Reformation lay piety. His father had initiated proceedings for the foundation of this college before his death in 1513, leaving his son to bring the project to fruition five years later. In 1518 Gerald petitioned William Rokeby, Archbishop of Dublin, for licence to establish and endow a college at Maynooth, his father having designated certain lands in County Meath for that purpose. By 12 October 1521 the archbishop had granted Gerald a licence for the project to go ahead along with a number of privileges relating to its administration. In that same year Gerald rebuilt the old thirteenth-century church of St Mary's which was attached to his castle at Maynooth and refurbished and adapted it in a very beautiful manner to serve as the new college's chapel. He then endowed the college with more generous possessions than he had at first intended. Gerald was reputed to have been especially devout; indeed, Stanihurst alleged: 'He is so religious addicted to the serving of God, as what time so ever he travelled to any part of the country, such as were of his chapel should be sure to accompany him.'[12]

Some ambiguity surrounds the exact function of the 'college'. The historian H. F. Hore claimed that the college was not an establishment for the provision of education for lay students; rather, it was conceived as a residence for a congregation of religious men. The Geraldine college was a chantry endowment, founded with the expressed purpose of housing clerics who would offer daily prayers for the souls of Gerald and his ancestors. As such, it was not an exceptional project by contemporary standards, as several other families in the Pale had made provision for similar, though more modest, endowments. While it would have been very exceptional in the Irish context for the college to have provided secular education, that possibility cannot categorically be discounted, particularly since similar chantry endowment colleges in England provided education for lay students even though their foundation charters (like that of the college at Maynooth) made no reference to their fulfilment of such a role.

The regulations for appointment of personnel show a definite delineation between secular and ecclesiastical administration. Moreover, this indicates Archbishop Rokeby's determination to ensure that Gerald would be prevented from establishing a monopoly of control over the college. Rokeby had no intention of allowing the college to become subsumed into the temporal jurisdiction of the earl's liberty of Kildare. Thus junior personnel such as the under-master and the boys were to be nominated by the earl, while the appointment of priests and receipt of temporality payments were to be the charge of the Archbishop of Dublin. Nonetheless, given that this was Gerald's endowment, it is not surprising that a compromise was reached between the two parties in the selection of clerical personnel, and the appointment of Edward Dillon as prebendary of Larabryne (Maynooth) provides evidence of such mutual accommodation, since Dillon was a close acquaintance of the Fitzgerald family. Although the college had a very short life (1521–38), eventually being suppressed along with all of the other County Kildare monastic houses in the late 1530s, its conception testifies to the fact that the leading family in the lordship, like other influential Pale families, was prepared to show initiative and generosity in sponsoring a large-scale project without any impetus from clerical authorities, and that they were thus far from lapsing into indifference in their piety.[13]

Such security as the ninth earl might have enjoyed in the midst of his lordship was, however, persistently challenged from without. Even in the era of the old earl there had been indications of rising discontent among the neighbouring Gaelic lordships. This was most obvious in 1510 when the eighth earl was compelled to mount an attack on Turlough Donn O'Brien and his allies outside Limerick and was subjected to a demoralising defeat by what he would have regarded as a Gaelic lord of mediocre standing. O'Brien's victory is generally regarded as something of a watershed in the history of the Kildare ascendancy, being interpreted as the incident which shattered the notion of the earl's military predominance. His failure to take O'Carroll's castle at Lemyvannan in 1513 marked a final admission of his decline.[14]

When John Kite arrived in Ireland in May 1514 to take up his appointment as Archbishop of Armagh, he reported finding 'disorder and licence' all around him. Neighbouring Gaelic septs made renewed and regular raids into the Pale, as well as seizing lands around its periphery. Steven Ellis suggests that in the eyes of the Gaelic lords, the Kildare ascendancy was very similar to those established by chiefs such as O'Neill and MacMurrough, and that it is likely that the Leinster septs made no real distinction between their loyalty to Kildare as overlord on the one hand and to the king in the person of Lord Deputy Kildare on the other.[15] It was therefore only to be expected that the newly succeeded ninth earl, both in his capacity as Lord Deputy and as overlord, would be subjected to similar tests of strength at the hands of Leinster septs as had to be endured by new incumbents of contested chieftaincies in Gaelic lordships.

He set about asserting his authority as overlord and as Lord Deputy by the traditional means of consolidating and developing traditional associations with Gaelic lords throughout the country, renewing existing agreements drawn up between the latter and his predecessors in a manner that was particularly effective in subjugating the fractious midland Gaelic chieftaincies.[16] In the case of more truculent vassals, he resorted to military campaigns. For example, in 1514 he plundered the territory of O'More in Leix and also led an army against O'Reilly in Breifne, in the north-west, destroying Cavan Castle and killing O'Reilly and many other notable figures in O'Reilly country.[17] In that same year he led an expedition into Munster where he was in contest with the joint forces of the Earl of Desmond's son and O'Brien.[18] Two years later, in an assault on O'Carroll's patrimony, Gerald succeeded where his father had previously failed in capturing Lemyvannan Castle in Offaly.[19] In 1518 he campaigned in Ulster, leading an army into Tyrone and demolishing the O'Neills' fortress at Dungannon.[20] Throughout the 1520s and early 1530s Kildare continued to engage in similar forays into Gaelic parts, impressing his authority as Lord Deputy and as overlord on lesser opponents.[21]

Between 1513 and 1519 Gerald governed in a manner similar to his father, while Henry VIII remained attentive but largely aloof from involvement in the administration of the lordship. Just how much free rein Kildare was afforded by Henry VIII in his governorship during the period 1513–19 is evidenced by the fact that Kildare had all money receipts, including the parliamentary subsidy which paid for the upkeep of the colony's administration and defence, conveyed directly to his own treasury. Yet this was never investigated until his successor, the Earl of Surrey, was appointed in 1520. The only significant new feature of Anglo-Irish relations was Henry VIII's practice of conferring Irish offices as rewards for his courtiers.[22] However, this was to have little tangible impact on Kildare's monopoly of control over the Irish council during those early years.

The year 1515, however, witnessed a brief though significant disruption of this favourable situation with the appearance of a serious body of criticism emerging from the inner circles of the Dublin administration itself. The principal spokesman of this group was William Darcy, Deputy Treasurer between 1504 and 1513, who had been removed from office and from the baronial council by Kildare. Darcy availed of Kildare's presence at court in April 1515, where the earl was concluding business concerning his inheritance and preparing for a forthcoming parliament, to present to the king and council a serious indictment of Kildare's conduct as governor. In his 'Articles on the Decay of Ireland' Darcy laid the blame for that decay at the feet of the Kildares by virtue of their pursuit of dynastic aggrandisement, and also at those of the king for his neglect of the lordship, both of which had caused the alleged contraction in the size of the colony. Kildare, he alleged, was seeking to usurp complete military, judicial and fiscal powers from the crown within his own earldom (as indeed were the Earls of Desmond and Ormond in their respective earldoms), and he warned that the earl's aim was to eventually annex the four Pale shires to his jurisdiction. Darcy particularly singled out for special censure Kildare's unlawful imposition of coign and livery on the colonists, his embarking on military campaigns without the prior consent of the Irish council, and his apparent leanings towards gaelicisation.[23] Unless Kildare changed his policies and his style of government, Darcy concluded, he ought to be removed from office and replaced by a governor who would be more sensitive and effective in protecting the interests of the colonists and of the king.

On this first occasion, however, such criticisms met with an indifferent response from Henry VIII. The king dismissed the complaints, and in a show of support for the earl he immediately affirmed his confidence in Kildare as deputy, while also enhancing his position both as deputy and as magnate. Henry authorised Gerald's confirmation as deputy with a commission which was as broad-ranging in its powers as Sir Edward Poynings' had been in 1494. A further demonstration of the king's confidence in Kildare was his granting him licence to table his own bills at a parliamentary session which was convened in February 1516 soon after his return from England. (Among these bills was one granting liberty status to the earl's Kildare patrimony, though it is not known whether this bill was in fact passed.)[24] The king also sanctioned his proposal to found and endow a college at Maynooth.[25]

Historians differ in their interpretation of the significance of this episode, some seeing it as proof that under Kildare the interests of the crown and the Anglo-Irish colony were being subordinated to the dynastic ambitions of the Fitzgeralds themselves.[26] Colm Lennon, however, regards it as the first manifestation among the gentry and urban patrician ranks of the Pale and other English districts of a campaign which would become increasingly forceful thereafter.[27] Steven Ellis suggests that the handful of Englishmen appointed by Henry VII and Henry VIII to government positions in the lordship may have incited the Anglo-Irish gentry and merchants of the Pale and outlying districts to articulate their sense of dissatisfaction at the Kildares' exploitation of power at the expense of their interests.[28] Regardless of which interpretation one finds most plausible, the fact remains that in the immediate aftermath of this incident, Gerald's position as Lord Deputy seemed secure, and his affirmed authority appeared to silence any further criticism of his ministering the lordship.

On a different level, however, the first rumblings of what was to develop into a major feud between the Kildare and Ormond dynasties manifested themselves late in that same year and reached a climax in July of the following year when Gerald received a letter from Henry VIII instructing him to lend his assistance to the seventh Earl of Ormond's daughters, Margaret Boleyn and Anne St Leger, in prosecuting their claim to the Ormond inheritance against the earl's cousin, Sir Piers Roe Butler of Polestown. It was a worrying development for Kildare, since it heralded the reawakening of disturbances in the Ormond territory which had been effectively calmed since 1497 with the death of Black James Butler. The king's expression of interest in the case also brought pressure to bear on Fitzgerald, whose loyalties were decidedly split on the issue. A former ally of Piers Roe, Kildare also stood to gain from the uncontested succession of a resident earl in the Ormond lordship, since he would thus be divested of responsibility for Kilkenny and Tipperary, an onerous task with which he had been saddled since his succession to the earldom in 1513.[29] Yet Kildare was also aware that support for Piers Roe's claim was likely to lose him favour with the king, for Margaret's son, Sir Thomas Boleyn, had close ties with Henry and his court, and the king was romantically involved with both his daughters, Mary and Anne.

Moves towards a temporary resolution of the problem came in December 1515 when the king granted livery of the Ormond inheritance in England, Wales and Ireland to the two Ormond heiresses. In Ireland the Earl of Kildare and the council recognised Piers Roe's claim, and in April 1516 he was granted livery of the Irish inheritance. Further rounds of legal wrangling ensued, the eventual outcome being that Piers Roe retained most of the Ormond holdings in Ireland, while the heiresses maintained custody of the dynasty's estates in England. The case rested so for the time being, only to re-emerge in 1526 when the king refused to recognise Piers as Earl of Ormond. However, in spite of Kildare's having afforded him his support, Piers evidently felt that his brother-in-law could have done a lot more to advance his claim had he wished to. Further tensions occurred as a result of Piers's refusal to compensate Kildare for the two-thirds of the income from the Ormond estates which both he and his father had received while the seventh Earl of Ormond was an absentee. An additional source of ill-feeling arose when a former member of the Dublin administration, Robert Cowley, whom Kildare had dismissed, tendered his services to Piers Roe, who used this lawyer's legal expertise and animosity towards Kildare to convey complaints against the deputy to the king, perhaps in the hope that he might secure royal recognition of his title in return for such loyal service.[30] Before 1520 Piers and Kildare had quarrelled, and the long-term implications of their falling-out were grave.

Even before that breach was final, however, a third and more significant challenge had arisen to Kildare's position. In January 1519, while undergoing a sudden awakening of interest in matters of state, Henry summoned Kildare to court to discuss the persistent complaints presented by the Anglo-Irish advocates of reform regarding the earl's alleged abuse of his power. Kildare clearly retained the king's confidence, since he was permitted to nominate his uncle, Maurice Fitzgerald of Lackagh, as his deputy during his absence. But an important change of atmosphere was taking place in Kildare's relations with the crown even as he took ship for England in September 1519.

3

KILDARE–ORMOND RIVALRY, THOMAS CROMWELL AND THE WEAKENING OF GERALDINE AUTONOMY, 1520–33

Soon after Gerald arrived in England Henry VIII and his council launched a debate on 'how Ireland may be reduced and restored to good order and obedience'.[1] The result was Kildare's dismissal and his replacement by Thomas Howard, Earl of Surrey, who came to Ireland holding the more prestigious title of Lord Lieutenant. On his arrival in May 1520, he was immediately confronted with glaring signs of the lordship's having fallen into a state of chronic decline. The evidence for Kildare's failure in government was weighty: he had even allowed Dublin Castle to decline into such a ruinous state that it was unfit for Surrey to occupy upon his arrival in the country. The records of the administration were in chaos, which necessarily impeded government. Surrey's Under-Treasurer, Sir John Stile, could find neither revenue nor evidence of any effort to collect it. It appeared that the only problem which could not be attributed to Kildare's maladministration was the ravages of plague which gripped the city of Dublin and the surrounding areas in 1520.

In accordance with his brief, Surrey engaged in three campaigns throughout the summer and autumn months, moving northwards against Conn Bacach O'Neill, into the midlands against O'More, and finally southwards to Waterford. Surrey retained the support of Piers Roe Butler, and his Ormond supporters, as well as the backing of careerist officials in the Dublin administration. But he was kept occupied in meeting the demands of everyday administrative matters and had little opportunity to attend to the fundamental problems impeding effective royal government. As early as July he was writing to Henry advising him that the reduction of Gaelic Ireland would necessitate a great force of men, money and the political commitment of the king to ensure its completion. Henry, however, quickly shrank away from committing himself to any of these. He sought a swift victory and the effective subjugation of the lordship with a view towards bolstering his standing in Europe in 1520. However, the expense which he incurred in his involvement in the Field of the Cloth of Gold, his alliance with Charles V in August and the approach of war with France effectively distracted him from Ireland. Deprived of the king's wholehearted support, Surrey's task was rendered all the more difficult by Kildare's resort to measures to secure his own position in the colony, in spite of his enforced absence.

Though put under obligation not to travel beyond London without permission, in June Kildare accompanied Henry VIII to the Field of the Cloth of Gold ceremony in France, where Kildare is said to have distinguished himself by his brilliant bearing.[2] In July, however, Kildare was awaiting interrogation by Wolsey, under threat that 'if he be found culpable in the crimes and offences laid to his charge' he would be punished so severely 'that all other shall take fearful example of him, sembably to offend hereafter'.[3] The case against Kildare was boosted by Surrey's report of a letter Kildare had written to O'Carroll expressing his pleasure at O'Carroll's behaviour during his absence and assuring him that 'whenever I come into Ireland, I shall do you good for anything that ye shall do for me'. He interceded with O'Carroll 'to keep good peace to Englishmen till an English deputy shall come thither; do your best to make war upon Englishmen then, except such as be toward me'.[4] Surrey was unable to secure possession of the letter in question, but alleged that Kildare had sent a similar letter to O'Neill. Although Kildare was briefly imprisoned, Henry's recognition that there were 'no evident testimonies' ensured his release. Yet Kildare remained under suspicion.

In spite of his absence, Kildare's behind-the-scenes activity determined the outcome of Surrey's lieutenancy in two key respects. Firstly, his inciting his Gaelic allies to stir up trouble for Surrey served to confirm the lieutenant and his council in their view that their existing resources were insufficient to see their plans for reform of the lordship through to fruition. Secondly, his continued assertion of his standing within the Pale resulted in a split emerging in the ranks of both the Gaelic Irish and the Pale aristocracy, between those who supported him in anticipation of his return and those who sought to advance their careers through adherence to the new regime. By December 1520 Surrey's despondency was evident. He declared that if Henry was unwilling to proceed with the conquest which he had advocated, then he was wasting his time and the king's money in continuing his service in Ireland. In the winter months of 1520–21 continental diplomacy took on a very different character: the diplomatic peace orchestrated by Wolsey in 1518 began to disintegrate, with Charles V and Francis I becoming poised for war and Henry VIII ranging himself on the side of Charles. Closer to home, the expiry of an Anglo-Scottish alliance agreement was accompanied by a looming threat of a Scottish invasion of Ireland, led by the Earl of Argyll. However, Henry was convinced that the Scots were most likely to mount their invasion through an assault on the northern marches of England, and thus he diverted his attention to securing the realm's defences in that region. The king was therefore more intent upon 'the advancement of other higher enterprises' than he was upon supporting Surrey's grandiose schemes for the subjugation of Gaelic Ireland.[5] Exasperated by his inability to galvanise Henry VIII into providing more reinforcements to enable him to administer the lordship more effectively, Surrey was even driven to requesting that Kildare be sent back to Ireland. By the spring of 1521 Henry confirmed his withdrawal from a commitment to the large-scale reform proposals which Surrey had formulated a year earlier. Surrey was advised to concentrate upon defending the Pale and on raising alternative revenues for the Dublin administration. As High Admiral of England, Surrey was eventually, and to his great relief, recalled from Ireland in September 1521 in order that he might serve in the war against France.

Although Surrey's lieutenancy in Ireland yielded few advances of royal power in the lordship, it served to weaken Kildare's position in the long term in two important respects. Firstly, Surrey's appointment signified the end of the quarter-century domination of the Earls of Kildare in the Dublin administration. Gerald was shown to be dispensable and was forced to resort to inciting his allies to put pressure on the colony's defences in an effort to counter this impression. Secondly, Henry's appointment of Surrey was greeted with hope and encouragement by the Anglo-Irish community, particularly by its advocates of reform, as they interpreted the change of governor as an indication of the king's lasting commitment to the lordship. Those advocates of reform were, of course, among Kildare's most censorious critics, and their growing confidence and success in gaining a hearing at the English court heralded inevitable conflict with Kildare's endeavours to retain his ascendant position in the Dublin government. Thus Kildare gradually began to appear as the principal obstacle to reform.[6] In the meantime, however, his marriage brought him into the fold of the influential Dorset court faction and did something to preserve his standing at court.

Yet Henry refused to consider the reinstatement of the earl to the vacant position of Lord Deputy of Ireland, despite the attractiveness of reverting to a financially self-sufficient style of aristocratic government. Other factors militated against his reversion to dependence on the earl's governance. Henry had committed himself to several members of the Pale community in stating that Kildare would not be restored. The king also viewed Kildare as causing factional disagreements with the Butlers and other Anglo-Irish and was aware of his implication in inciting assaults on the Pale as shows of his indispensability during his absence in London. Moreover, Henry was also loath to admit that his initial decision to remove Kildare from office had been an error of judgement. Wolsey's rejection of Surrey's suggestion that the earl be reinstated undoubtedly confirmed him in his decision to look for an alternative to Kildare in his appointment of Surrey's successor. Yet, while Henry was not prepared to engage in serious involvement in Ireland, he was determined not to allow the lordship to sink into faction and widespread disorder or to retrench from exerting a continuous influence in the conduct of government there.[7] Thus, in a move designed to prove his determination to govern the lordship without Kildare, Henry appointed Sir Piers Roe Butler as Lord Deputy, Butler having been acting as deputy lieutenant to Surrey since December 1521.

Butler, whose claim to the title of Earl of Ormond was not recognised by Henry VIII, was installed on 26 March 1522. From the outset of his term of office Henry sought to restrict Ormond's grip on the Dublin administration by reserving to himself the right to nominate the eight principal officials of the government. He immediately deprived Ormond's administration of English subventions, forcing Ormond to harness his own resources to bolster the paltry returns yielded by the Irish revenues which went nowhere near meeting the costs of administration and defence of the colony. Given the remoteness of his estates from the Pale marchlands, Ormond proved incapable of pacifying or suppressing the Gaelic septs, some of whom were Kildare's allies, who continued to mount raids on the Pale. Kildare, by contrast, had shown himself capable of providing unequalled protection of the Pale through his success in controlling these septs in the past.

Faced with these insurmountable odds, Ormond, like his predecessor Surrey, soon requested Kildare's return to the lordship in order to defend his lands on the Pale frontier and to exert his controlling influence over his fractious kinsmen and allies. By the end of April 1522 Ormond had learned that Kildare was to be permitted to return home, and on 1 January 1523 Gerald arrived in Ireland, accompanied by his new wife, after an absence of almost three and a half years. He did so with both Henry's and Wolsey's expressed instruction that he pacify his own territory of Kildare and that he co-operate with Ormond in the defence of the colonists' interests. Not all of his family, however, were pleased by Kildare's return: several of his uncles, brothers and cousins initially proved less than enthusiastic, though most of them were eventually rallied by a reassertion of their family loyalty.[8] The most serious problem facing him was the continuation of the feud with Sir Piers Butler, now made graver by Ormond's conduct during Kildare's absence at court.

Right from the time of his arrival in Ireland, Kildare proved himself unwilling to reach a *modus vivendi* with Ormond. He adamantly refused to acquiesce to his position of subordination to Ormond, who held the position to which he felt he had a virtual hereditary claim. The two earls very soon became locked in conflict which was to persist throughout the 1520s and early 1530s. Kildare was quick to launch his offensive against Ormond, alleging that the Lord Deputy neglected his council. He was also likely to have been actively engaged in conspiring with old official families in Dublin, members of the Pale gentry, to undermine Ormond's authority. What is certain is that Kildare acted as though he himself were deputy, leading an army comprised of his tenants and allies into Ulster without seeking any prior clearance from Ormond. Although he claimed that his expedition was undertaken to protect his lands in the old Ulster earldom, Kildare's real motive was to launch a full-scale attack on O'Neill of Clandeboy, as well as on Scottish forces in Ulster and on the town of Carrickfergus.[9] The risk deepened in May 1523 when Kildare complained to Henry VIII about Ormond, charging him with capitalising on his absence in Ulster through the seizure of several castles in the marchlands.

But the dispute reached its climax over the matter of the levying of troops and supplies in County Kildare. The core of the conflict was the question of whether Kildare would permit Ormond to levy coign and livery within his Kildare liberty, and whether Ormond would recognise Kildare's claim to impose coign and livery for his own private purposes within Kildare or elsewhere. By the summer of 1523 allegations and counter-allegations were being forwarded to the court on both earls' parts, with their countesses making representation on behalf of their husbands. Weary of this constant litany of complaints and allegations emanating from the lordship, Henry VIII decided to intervene to resolve the dispute. He appointed an arbitration council comprised of the lordship's leading archbishops, George Cromer, Archbishop of Armagh, and Hugh Inge, Archbishop of Dublin, the Treasurer, Sir John Rawson, and the Chief Justice of the King's Bench, Patrick Bermingham. On 28 November they presented their formula for an agreement. Ormond was entitled to his official right to impose coign and livery in Kildare, while Gerald was permitted the unofficial privilege of imposing similar exactions in Kildare, though these were to be exacted on a 'voluntary' basis by the earl. Kildare was granted an annuity of £100 to help defray some of the cost of defending the Pale. However, this settlement was soon overturned by the murder of Robert Talbot, Sheriff of County Dublin, by Kildare's brother James, while the sheriff was *en route* to Kilkenny to spend Christmas with Ormond.[10]

Throughout the early months of 1524 both earls intensified their efforts to discredit the other, increasingly harnessing the intervention of influential faction leaders at the court to secure the advancement of their respective cause. Kildare used his connections with Dorset and with Surrey, whom he had befriended since the latter's sojourn in Ireland. Ormond persuaded his son James, who was resident at court, to represent his case. In response to their representations, and aware of the detrimental impact of this feuding on the Pale community in particular, Henry appointed an arbitration commission to settle all disputes in the Pale and specifically that between Kildare and Ormond. In June commissioners were sent with a brief to involve Kildare more directly in government, and indeed to arrange a transfer of authority from Ormond to Kildare if they regarded this as a justifiable step. On 12 July they summoned an assembly of landholders in the Pale and surrounding districts and had them submit to enter into agreements to regulate their means of mustering troops, and a grand agreement was devised to resolve the dispute between Kildare and Ormond.

The two earls each gave bonds of 1,000 Irish marks before the Irish council to adhere to the terms of this agreement. They undertook to support the king's ministers, to uphold the king's law, and not to billet any more troops on the lordship than was absolutely necessary for defence. As a show of his earnest intention to adhere to the terms of this agreement, Kildare entrusted his brother James to the charge of the three commissioners, and James was thereafter led through the streets of London with a noose around his neck before eventually being pardoned.[11]

Kildare formally took up his duties as Lord Deputy on 4 August 1524 at a ceremony held in Christ Church which was followed by a banquet in Thomas Court. Among those present was Conn Bacach O'Neill, whose attendance is thought to have been deliberately arranged by Kildare as a ploy to demonstrate publicly the high esteem in which he was held by one of the most formidable Gaelic lords.[12] At the same time Ormond was appointed Treasurer. However, Gerald soon found that his tenure of the post to which he was restored was significantly altered in comparison with his term of office before his dismissal in 1520. His position was increasingly under scrutiny from London, particularly as relations between himself, Ormond and Desmond grew more tense as the years passed.[13] According to the terms of the reconciliation agreement, Kildare was limited in the extent to which he could levy exactions for military campaigns within the Pale and expenses for more long-distance forays. He was also bound to permit the courts and local officials of the crown such as justices of the peace to function independently of any interference on his part. Moreover, he gave an undertaking to heed the advice of his council in his governance and to set aside his grievances with Ormond, Sir William Darcy and others. But no sooner had the commissioners departed Ireland in September 1524 than it began to become evident that the reconciliation would not last. The council reported that Kildare seemed more agreeable than Ormond had been, but its members trusted neither earl.[14] Kildare immediately set about curbing Ormond's influence in the administration by appointing one of his own supporters, Lord Trimbleston, as Under-Treasurer.

In the short term, however, relations between the earls seemed less overtly antagonistic than they had done previously, though that was for reasons of self-interest rather than any evidence of their grappling to remain committed to the agreement. Gerald was preoccupied with his endeavours to reassert his authority within his liberty of Kildare, where he had to contend with family members who had appropriated some of his lands and authority during his absence in London.[15] His reinstatement brought peace and order to the Pale to the extent that he was now able to concentrate on resuming his involvement in Gaelic lordships. He channelled much of his energy into reestablishing his alliances with the Gaelic Irish, particularly O'Neill and O'Donnell, both of whom he induced to attend a meeting of the council in Dublin at this time. In 1524 he led a hosting against O'Donnell and another foray into Connacht in 1526. At this time Kildare found it difficult to depend on several of his Gaelic allies and was forced to withstand harassment within his own liberty of Kildare at the hands of the O'Mores.[16] This need to constantly exert influence in Gaelic circles was clearly recognised by Kildare and by his contemporaries as being a fundamental dimension to his dynasty's political ascendancy, yet the earl was well aware that there was only so much that he could expect to achieve through such sporadic campaigns.[17] Ormond was similarly engaged in strengthening his position in Kilkenny, and neither earl paid much attention to ominous events which were afoot in Desmond's lordship at this time and which were to cause their feud to reignite.

THE WEAKENING OF GERALDINE AUTONOMY, 1520-33   41

In the late summer of 1524 Ormond was finding it difficult to supervise the Earl of Desmond's manoeuvres. Desmond exploited Ormond's quarrel with Kildare by raiding Ormond's estates in Tipperary and capitalised on dissent among the junior branches of the Butler family in an effort to undermine the earl's position. With Kildare constantly attacking the northern quarters of his estate, Ormond felt seriously threatened by Geraldine alliances on two separate fronts, and he therefore alleged to the king that both Geraldine earls were united in a conspiracy against the crown. Kildare denied the charge of complicity with Desmond in his intrigues with agents sent to Kerry by Francis I. He urged Henry VIII 'not to regard such untrue surmises of mine adversaries' and emphasised that 'I never did, nay thought, anything, whereby I should deserve your . . . displeasure'.[18] But Kildare's stand in the controversy was undermined by his failure as Lord Deputy to apprehend Desmond. He was reluctant to campaign against Desmond in Munster, thereby placing Ormond at a distinct advantage over him and leaving his own bulwark of Kildare open to assault by Ormond's allies, the O'Carrolls. By the time he eventually led an army into Munster, Desmond had already ensured his evasion of possible capture, refusing to meet with Kildare on the grounds of claiming his privilege to absent himself from parliament and walled towns.[19] Kildare's sudden shift of attention to Tyrconnell, which he invaded in alliance with Conn Bacach O'Neill, undoubtedly aggravated Ormond, further convincing him of the Lord Deputy's indifference to Desmond's posturing.

Once again the litany of charges and counter-charges was revived between the two earls as viciously as in the past. Ormond accused Kildare of being in breach of the terms of the 1524 agreement since he was imposing intolerable military exactions on the Pale community and was allegedly inciting Gaelic septs to mount attacks against Ormond. He claimed that Kildare had engaged the O'Byrnes to assist Desmond at a time when the latter was intriguing with Charles V. He alleged that Kildare had armed the Irish against his own authority as Lord Deputy and that he had executed good subjects of the king merely because they were adherents of the Butlers. Kildare, on the other hand, insisted that Ormond was imposing similar exactions in his territories in

Kilkenny and Tipperary, as well as inciting his allies to attack Kildare's tenants and allies within County Kildare.[20] Kildare even raked up accusations regarding Ormond's alleged misbehaviour as far back as 1516. This mutual defamation continued throughout 1525 and early 1526. Given the continental dimension to Desmond's intrigue which had sparked the revival of the Kildare–Ormond feud, Henry VIII was galvinised into taking direct steps to secure an agreement between the two earls. Only by doing so could he hope to put paid to Desmond's plans, restore order to the lordship and eliminate the threat of continental intervention in Ireland as a step towards undermining the Tudor regime.[21] Whereas previously Henry had sent arbitrators to Ireland in an effort to reach a lasting agreement, on this occasion he summoned the two earls to his court in August 1526 in an effort to persuade them to work together to end Desmond's intrigue.

Ormond proved compliant with the royal summons, immediately travelling to London in a conscious step to arrive before his rival. Kildare, by contrast, delayed his departure in order to put in place a number of measures designed to secure his position during his indefinite absence. The most important of these was his nomination of Sir Thomas Fitzgerald of Leixlip as his deputy. He then travelled to England before the end of 1526. Henry VIII's council found it impossible to make any assessment of the earls' positions based upon the teeming collection of accusations with which they were presented. Kildare was not cleared of Ormond's accusations, but Surrey, by this time created Duke of Norfolk, offered to receive the earl into his home during his detention in England. However, Norfolk stressed that Kildare would eventually have to be sent back to Ireland. An attempt was also made to avail of this opportunity to tackle the problem of the controversial Ormond succession to lands and titles, but this was not achieved until 1528.

In contrast with his rival, Piers Roe Butler, who showed his resourcefulness in adapting the pursuit of his interests to Henry VIII's wishes in order to retain the king's favour, Kildare exhibited no such flexibility during his interrogations by Wolsey and continued to be detained as a result. Wolsey is said to have been incensed by Gerald's manner of responding to his interrogation and duly imprisoned the earl and deferred his case until such time as more concrete incriminating information was forthcoming from Ireland.[22]

Stanihurst's coloured version of the encounter is nonetheless revealing, for it makes clear that even at this stage Kildare would make no apology for his resort to extra-judicial methods to suppress disturbances. His case rested on the premise that the only alternative to a 'new conquest' (which he knew Henry VIII would not be prepared to fund) was to allow the Anglo-Irish aristocracy, headed by Kildare himself, to exercise their discretion in maintaining the peace and in administering justice in their immediate sphere. Implicit in Kildare's argument was the belief that capturing Desmond and violently reducing Gaelic septs would not be necessary if the system of private jurisdiction which he advocated were allowed to operate fully—with his own personal power, of course, being at the centre of such a system.

Kildare's removal from Ireland for another three and a half years until 1530, combined with Ormond's absence during part of that time, resulted in escalating disorder in the Pale and outlying areas in this period. Kildare pointed to the extremely disturbed state of the lordship during his enforced absence, portraying this as conclusive proof of his dynasty's unique capacity to govern Ireland in the name of the king. While not all of the problems experienced by the lordship could be attributed to Gerald's absence, there were some grounds for his assertion of his indispensability to effective government. The taxpayers of the colony at large only appeared to have been agreeable to paying subsidies to a Geraldine administration, with little enthusiasm being displayed for innovative methods of raising funds to implement reforms. Kildare alone seemed strong enough to be able to inflict punishment on troublesome Gaelic lords in the border regions through his policy of 'knee-cutting' and his relentless prosecution of those who were found to be in breach of his 'slantyaght'. It appears, therefore, that in the late 1520s both the colonists and the Gaelic Irish had become well accustomed to aristocratic government, that they had a reluctant preference for Geraldine control of the deputyship, and that attempts to introduce any alternative approach to government would prove very difficult to realise.[23]

During Kildare's absence Sir Thomas Fitzgerald of Leixlip appears to have co-operated fully with the Dublin council in efforts to organise the defence of the Pale throughout 1526 and the early months of the following year. However, he was convinced that he did not have the full backing of all of the members of the council, and consequently he resigned his post before 14 September 1527, probably at the king's prompting.[24] Sir Thomas was replaced by the veteran captain and ally of the Butlers, Richard Nugent, Lord Delvin, a native of Westmeath, whose appointment is regarded as signalling the determination of Westmeath's lesser magnates to throw off the shackles of Fitzgerald domination to which they had been subjected since the 1490s. Delvin was unable to contend with persistent raids mounted by O'Neill and O'Connor Faly at Kildare's councillors' instigation 'in the hope that he should the rather come home'.[25] Wolsey was informed by Archbishop Inge and Chief Justice Bermingham that 'the vice-deputy is not of power to defend the Englishry, and yet the poor people is far more charged and oppressed by him than they have been, the Earl of Kildare being here'.[26] In the spring of 1528 Sir Piers Butler, now holding the title Earl of Ossory (by which title he will henceforth be referred to), was permitted to return to Ireland, while Kildare was still detained.

Kildare's offensive was stepped up in May 1528 when his supporters, including Sir Thomas of Leixlip and the earl's daughter Alice, conspired to have Delvin kidnapped by Kildare's son-in-law, O'Connor of Offaly, and held him in captivity for several months.[27] His ransom was a demand for restoration of the subsidy for the upkeep of the administration and the army and the return of Kildare to Ireland. The Dublin government was plunged into chaos by the deputy's abduction, and the Geraldine plot was successful to a point, in that it forced the council to appoint Sir Thomas Fitzgerald as general captain of the greater Pale area since the members were convinced that 'the strength, if any be, is by the Geraldines'.[28]

In spite of the fact that James Butler alleged that the kidnapping was orchestrated by 'the Earl of Kildare's councillors, and band', the Irish council requested either Kildare's return or substantial military reinforcement to tackle this crisis.[29] Henry, however, refused to succumb to the councillors' pressure either to pay for an enlarged army or to reinstate Kildare, for he was convinced that Kildare had orchestrated these disturbances in order to 'fraudulently . . . colour that the king should think that [he] could not be served there, but only by' Kildare.[30] Henry's resolve was no doubt strengthened when it emerged that Kildare had sent a letter to his daughter in Ireland, Lady Slane, in July 1528, wherein he urged his nephew, Conn Bacach O'Neill, and his son-in-law, O'Connor, to invade the Pale. As a result of this discovery, Kildare was again imprisoned.[31] Notwithstanding his profound dislike of Kildare, Wolsey urged Henry not to remove Gerald from the office of Lord Deputy for a number of reasons, the most important of which was his conviction that as long as Kildare was deputy, his kinsmen and allies were afraid that any damage done by them might be laid to Kildare's charge. But the king also rejected Wolsey's suggested strategy of appointing Ossory as deputy to Kildare during the latter's continued detention in England. Ignoring Norfolk's advice that Ossory would be incapable of defending the Pale, Henry appointed a reluctant Ossory to the post of Lord Deputy in August 1528. Thus Kildare's strategy ultimately failed to secure the intended response, namely his own reinstatement as deputy.

Following Ossory's appointment, Kildare was released on bail, with a host of influential courtiers acting as security for him. He then took up residence in the Duke of Norfolk's home at Newington in Middlesex.[32] Meanwhile, although Ossory managed to restore some semblance of order in the southern parts of the Irish lordship, by the spring of 1529 he was complaining of the pro-Geraldine character of the Irish council and appealed for reinforcements to be dispatched from England to enable him to defend the Pale marches. Ossory testified to the formidable strength of the Geraldine party in the lordship, claiming that they had at their disposal a great retinue of 'men of war', strong garrisons, plenty of ammunition and a knowledge of the topography of the countryside, all of which enabled them to inflict more damage than three times as many in any other part of the realm. It was also alleged that Lady Slane had held a secret meeting with O'Connor, after which she 'made invasions, raids and hostilities'.[33]

By the summer of 1529 Ossory's manifest inadequacies in defending the Pale necessitated the king's intervention once again. Henry decided to release Ossory from the deputyship in June and to allow him to concentrate on pacifying the south of the lordship. There Ossory had been coming under pressure again from Desmond, who had won the support of malcontent Butlers and who was also actively engaged in conspiring with Charles V's envoy, Gonzalo Fernandez, in February 1529. Fortunately for Ossory and for the crown, the death of the eleventh Earl of Desmond resulted in the abandonment of continental intrigue and hostility towards Ossory.

Even though the crisis had passed in the Desmond lordship, in July 1529 Henry VIII dispatched his master of the ordnance, Sir William Skeffington, to Ireland, under instruction to report on the Irish military situation. In an unprecedented departure in terms of Tudor governance of the lordship, the king then proceeded to appoint his natural son, Henry Fitzroy, Duke of Richmond, as Lord Lieutenant of Ireland, with the task of actual government being entrusted to a 'secret council' comprising the new Chancellor and Archbishop of Dublin, John Alen, the Treasurer, John Rawson, and Chief Justice Patrick Bermingham.[34] This innovation formed part of Wolsey's grander scheme for the assimilation of regions such as the north of England and Wales in the mid-1520s. However, the king refused to provide the council with the requisite funds to enable its members to administer and defend the lordship adequately.[35] A final blow was dealt to the secret council's prospects when Archbishop Alen became discredited as a result of his association with the disgraced Cardinal Wolsey. Alen was dismissed from the chancellorship, and the commission fell to Rawson and Bermingham instead. The odds were steadily mounting in favour of Kildare's reappointment.

In June Henry decided to send Skeffington back to Ireland, this time as Lord Deputy. But with his appointment came another new departure in the crown's attempts to tackle the problem of governing the lordship: Kildare was finally to be allowed to return home and was to work in conjunction with this English Lord Deputy. The decision to allow Kildare to return was in response to pressure applied on his behalf by the influential Grey family and by the Earl of Wiltshire (Thomas Boleyn) at the court. It was also partly attributable to Norfolk's representations which sprang from his conviction that Kildare was a necessary evil which had to be tolerated if the king hoped to restore relatively inexpensive but effective government and defence of the country. Thus, frustrated at the failed outcome of successive strategies to govern without Kildare, yet intent upon not spending the requisite amount on furnishing troops and subsidies, Henry VIII aimed to test whether Kildare could deploy his personal resources and his grasp of *realpolitik* in restoring the government in the weakened lordship.[36]

On 24 August 1530 Skeffington, accompanied by Kildare, landed in Ireland and immediately divested the commissioners of the secret council of their duties. Backed by 200 troops, Skeffington was to fend off raids on the Pale. He was also charged to reconcile the outstanding differences between the Earls of Kildare, Ossory and Desmond, inducing all three to co-operate in order to restore peace and strong royal government in the lordship. He was to enjoy the active support of Kildare, who had given an undertaking 'to employ . . . himself . . . for the annoyance of the king's said rebellious subjects of the wild Irishry'.[37] To that end, the earl was permitted to have the use, on conditional and specific terms, of those English soldiers who were not engaged by Skeffington in active service at a given time. This was to enable him to fulfil his special role of pacifying the border chiefs in the outlying areas of the Pale. This strategy was rather naïve, since, as he had shown very clearly in the years 1524–6, Kildare was incapable of sharing power. Now he was expected to endure the indignity of being subordinate to a commoner 'of mean birth' who held the position of Lord Deputy to which Kildare felt he had a virtually automatic and sole right.

Initially, however, Kildare was clever in projecting himself as being entirely co-operative with the deputy. For almost a year Kildare and Skeffington campaigned both separately and jointly and in the process overcame opposition in the south, west and north of the Pale, subjugating O'Toole and O'More, and in the north secured submissions from O'Neill and O'Donnell. During the earl's absence in England, O'Toole had plundered his tenants, and Kildare therefore set out to punish the Gaelic lord, assisted by 200 archers from Dublin city bands of military forces.[38]

Whether these submissions can be attributed more to Kildare's association with Skeffington than to the deputy's military expertise is difficult to ascertain. However, those relations quickly turned sour by early summer 1531. The new administration under Skeffington's deputyship was proving comparatively expensive: by May 1531 Henry had spent almost £5,000. The king cut back his subvention, and consequently Skeffington was forced to scale down his army, a decision inspired by the fact that his billeting the troops on the citizens of Dublin had given rise to 'a great fray' between the inhabitants and his soldiers in July 1531.[39] By then Skeffington and Kildare had fallen out and the Kildare–Ormond feud raged once again, the latter development resulting from the Lord Deputy's deliberate efforts to rekindle the dormant dispute so as to enable him to exercise freedom of action. Indeed, it is suspected that Skeffington might have been engaged in encouraging some of Kildare's kinsmen and Gaelic allies to oppose the earl.

Bills tabled at Skeffington's two parliamentary sessions held in Dublin and Drogheda in the months of September and October 1531 respectively lent weight to Kildare's conviction that the deputy was seeking to stir antagonism between him and Ossory. A bill stipulated that lands of absentees in Counties Kildare, Carlow and west Wicklow which had been granted to Kildare's father and his heirs in 1482 were now to revert (if still waste land) to the representatives of their former owners. Inevitably this aroused Kildare's ire since Ossory would thus secure a base from which he could penetrate Kildare's immediate sphere of the liberty of Kildare. The other beneficiary from this bill was the newly appointed Archbishop of Dublin, John Alen, who also hoped to claw back properties rightfully belonging to the metropolitan see.[40] In spite of Skeffington's connivance, however, his deputyship was becoming increasingly redundant as Kildare mobilised support within the Irish council while simultaneously harnessing the support of his two influential court allies, Norfolk and Wiltshire. This is demonstrated by Ossory's sudden direction of his energies towards recovering his influence at the court, on this occasion developing contacts with the increasingly prominent Thomas Cromwell, further to his realisation that he had made a tactical error in backing Skeffington against an increasingly pro-Geraldine council. The message which he conveyed to Cromwell was that Skeffington was now very much under Kildare's control.[41]

In the eyes of the Irish council, Skeffington was seen to have been supporting Ossory against Kildare, while Ossory believed the opposite to be true. Early in 1532 Ossory accused Kildare of using his connections with Wiltshire to prejudice his claim to certain Butler lands in Tullow and Arklow to which he had a title. Moreover, he went on to accuse Kildare of inciting his relative, Sir Edmund Butler, to oppose him in Tipperary. He claimed that Kildare had 'displayed his standard' and mustered all of his forces in order to attack and plunder Ossory's territory.[42] In addition, he complained that Kildare had mistreated his retinue during a joint campaign against O'Neill and alleged that the earl had endeavoured to strengthen Desmond's resistance to the Butlers.

By April 1532 Skeffington's deputyship appeared doomed: complaints emanating from all parties in the lordship about his performance as deputy were directed to London. In response, Henry VIII summoned Kildare, Ossory's son James Butler, Rawson and Patrick Bermingham to be examined before the king's council at Greenwich in May regarding the behaviour of the two earls and the Lord Deputy.[43] The summons was partly motivated by Henry's displeasure at having spent a substantial amount in maintaining Skeffington and his troops for which the only return was a crescendo of complaints regarding the continual weakening of the lordship and little evidence of its pacification. Rawson and Bermingham confirmed Henry's assessment of the situation, advising him of Skeffington's failure to field his entire retinue and cavalry at a recent hosting and accusing the deputy of exploiting his position in order to pursue personal ends. They also accused him of grave financial malpractice, partiality, and of merely pretending to raise musters. Neither had Skeffington fulfilled one of his main charges, namely to quell the feud between Kildare and Ossory.

Skeffington's downfall was to prove Kildare's opportunity. Bermingham and Rawson exonerated Kildare, alleging that he had done the king good service until recently when he was provoked by Skeffington's favouritism towards Ossory. James Butler testified that Skeffington had been responsible for reigniting the Kildare–Ormond feud. Again at the urging of Gerald's court allies, Norfolk and Wiltshire, Henry dismissed Skeffington, and having concluded that the lordship could be governed more economically and effectively by Kildare, he reappointed the earl as deputy on 5 July 1532, 'thinking it expedient in so fickle a world to have a sure post in Ireland'.[44]

4

CROMWELLIAN REFORM AND THE GERALDINE REVOLT OF 1534

The most salient feature of royal policy towards Ireland during the 1520s and early 1530s was it weakness, due largely to the king's refusal to spend money on providing effective government and defence. Frequent changes of deputies resulted from inadequate support from the crown and led to a worsening of the administration's existing difficulties. As a result, as time passed, the lordship was governed less and less effectively but at greater cost to the royal exchequer.[1] Royal policy undoubtedly also weakened Gerald Fitzgerald's position, as the earl's concerted efforts to regain the coveted deputyship suggest. In outlying areas in England Henry sought to weaken the position of magnates by depriving them of offices which they traditionally occupied. Yet, in spite of being removed from office of Lord Deputy in the years 1520–24 and 1528–32, as well as being detained in England in 1519–23 and 1526–30, Kildare's personal absence from Ireland made a surprisingly small dent in his power. During the period 1520–32 there is no evidence of a consistent policy of royal supervision of the deputy: rather, Henry resorted to intermittent summoning of the deputy to London to answer charges levied against him. That the impact of royal policy on the government of the lordship was superficial during these twelve years is evidenced by the fact that Kildare retained a strong influence over the Irish council and over the officers of the administration. Indeed, so strong was that influence that Kildare's critics complained that the council had effectively been reduced to acting as a mouthpiece for the deputy. Many members of the council supported his policies, and those who did not could be induced to remain silent.

Even though Henry VIII reserved to himself the right to appoint senior members of the administration, Kildare still managed to ensure that a very substantial number of his supporters retained office, even while he was detained in England. The council therefore could not be relied upon during the period 1520–32 as a constraining agency on Kildare's power as deputy. In 1525 Ormond complained that Kildare had persuaded councillors to write letters of complaint about him to the king. Ormond also claimed that no one dared to criticise Kildare. Before his departure for London in 1526, having been summoned by Henry VIII, Kildare took an oath from each councillor, unknown to each other, that each would write to the king in his favour. Even as late as 1533 Kildare's critics complained that the Dublin council was 'partly corrupted with affection' towards the earl and 'partly in such dread of him that either they will not or dare not do any thing that should be displeasant to him'.[2]

Opinions differ as to whether Kildare's effectiveness in imposing order in the Pale was significantly weakened by his protracted absences, and this in turn has shaped historians' interpretation of the last two years of Kildare rule. On the one hand, the earl's campaigns are recorded in the annals for each year that he was resident in Ireland, and he continued to exert his authority over Gaelic septs who paid him for his protection.[3] Indeed, he successfully countered an attempt by O'Donnell to reach a settlement with the king by alleging that the Gaelic lord was not genuine in his submission.[4] On the other hand, there is evidence that Kildare's authority was on the wane from about December 1533. In the winter of 1532–3 he was engaged in mediating in a succession dispute among the O'Carrolls, and during the course of this campaign he gained possession of two castles. While besieging Birr Castle, Gerald was 'shot into the body with a handgun and not slain, but he was never whole again'.[5] His injury was kept secret until after the castle was taken by his forces, and only in the following spring was the shot removed from his side. As a result of this wound, Gerald partially lost the use of his limbs and his speech. Kildare's allies were also encountering serious difficulties in pursuing campaigns to reduce recalcitrant Gaelic septs. His brothers James, Richard and Walter were defeated in their raids on the O'Tooles, James only managing to escape 'by swiftness of his horse, his men slain', while the other two brothers 'escaped in the clothing of women'.[6] Soon afterwards another of Gerald's brothers, John Fitzgerald, launched an attack on the MacMahons, but was confronted, wounded and pursued for six miles with the loss of thirty of his men. Gerald's son, Thomas, Lord Offaly suffered defeat in a raid on O'Reilly in Breifne.[7] Around this time too the O'Byrnes raided Dublin Castle, released some of the prisoners and generally terrified the citizens in an embarrassing demonstration of Kildare's inability to defend the heart of the Pale.

It is important to note that Henry's concern to control Kildare was essentially reactive. Kildare was summoned to answer allegations of his abuse of power: there was never any question of his incompetence as Lord Deputy. Henry showed no sign of interest in a military conquest. Since he was unable to arrive at some alternative to either restoring Kildare with wide-ranging powers or appointing an English deputy backed by an expensive standing army, Henry opted for the former, seeing Kildare as the only man capable of commanding the support of Anglo-Irish and Gaelic Irish alike and restoring peace to the lordship.

In the summer months of 1532, therefore, there was little reason to suspect that within two years the king would be adopting a policy of sustained intervention in the government and defence of the lordship. Kildare's reappointment has been viewed by historians as a reversion to the position of 1524. His reinstatement was a tacit recognition by the crown of the earl's indispensability in the government of the lordship which resulted from Henry's unwillingness to send troops and money to fund an alternative to Kildare's governance. Kildare set about exacting retribution on his opponents soon after resuming office. He first targeted Skeffington: while mustering the latter's troops before their departure on campaign, Kildare publicly humiliated Skeffington, who was forced to suffer the added indignity of remaining on in the earl's service for two months after the incident. Skeffington withdrew to England, where he lent his voice to the Butlers' lobby against Kildare. Henry VIII had made no effort to secure a reconciliation between the two rivals, and their feud took a particularly malevolent turn by the end of 1532 when Piers Roe Butler's son Thomas was killed by Geraldine supporters. Kildare also launched a punitive attack on Piers Roe's territory and dispatched his brother John to co-operate with his cousin, Conn Bacach O'Neill, in raiding Louth.[8]

The story of the Geraldine rebellion has been the subject of varied interpretation both at the hands of the near-contemporary chronicler Richard Stanihurst and those of successive generations of historians. Writing in the 1570s while in the employment of the eleventh Earl of Kildare, Stanihurst attributed the outbreak of rebellion to conspiracies contrived by Kildare's opponents to remove him from the deputyship. Leading figures among these conspirators, he alleged, were the Earl of Ossory (Piers Roe Butler) and his supporters, the anti-Kildare cohort in the Dublin council and Sir William Skeffington, who worked to undermine Kildare from his base in England. The result of their endeavours was the circulation of a false report that the Earl of Kildare (who had been detained in England since early 1534, having been summoned there by Henry VIII) had been executed in London. But Stanihurst's account, while substantially factually accurate, nonetheless telescopes events. The chronicler creates an impression of a fast-paced, sudden, spontaneous reactive outburst by a young and impetuous Lord Offaly. Relying on Stanihurst's account, an older generation of historians tended to argue that the removal of Kildare from power in 1533 was the result of a long-term erosion of his power and that his dismissal heralded a new departure in crown policy, which now became one of conquest: thus the rebellion merely facilitated the implementation of this policy.

By contrast, the reality, as a number of recent historians have shown, was much more complex. Modern scholars stress the central role played by Henry VIII's secretary, Thomas Cromwell, though they differ in their estimation of his importance. Appointed in January 1533, Cromwell was instrumental in instituting administrative reforms which were not designed to destroy the Kildares but which nevertheless managed to achieve this outcome. By the time of his elevation Cromwell was very well briefed on issues relating to the Irish lordship: Ossory and Anglo-Irish critics of aristocratic rule in Ireland found in him a willing auditor and therefore supplied him with detailed critical reports on the state of Ireland during 1533 and 1534. The secretary's objectives were threefold: firstly, he sought to obtain impartial reports about Irish affairs; secondly, he encouraged direct communication between the Irish council and the king, thereby diminishing the role of the

Lord Deputy as intermediary; and lastly, he endeavoured to bring patronage in Ireland more tightly under royal control. In addition, Henry sought to cultivate the support of Kildare's own brothers in opposition to the earl.[9]

Cromwell's proposals for reform were outlined in his *Ordinances for the Government of Ireland* (1534). These were intended as a blueprint for the newly reformed government and were compiled as part of Cromwell's strategy of constitutional and administrative designs by which he sought to strengthen royal government in outlying areas of the realm. In essence they heralded the end of bastard feudalism in the colonial region of the lordship and provided for the revival of crown government.[10] Yet there was nothing especially new in the substance of these dictates, the only innovation being Cromwell's concerted bid to secure their observance by having them printed for wider circulation. The reality was that Cromwell appears to have had given little consideration to the manner in which he could implement these reforming notions. Consequently, it was not until after the outbreak of the Geraldine revolt that anything resembling a policy of reform actually began to emerge. By assuming authority in the dispensing of patronage, Cromwell aimed to cultivate independent politicians who had espoused a commitment to the advance of political reform in Ireland.

In the event, however, his intended refurbishment of the Irish council got no further than his appointment of one Butler supporter, Christopher Delahide, as a judge in the Court of King's Bench in 1533 and also his advance of a cousin and namesake of the Archbishop of Dublin, John Alen, to the position of Master of the Rolls. Controversy surrounded the appointment of a successor to the deceased Chief Justice of the King's Bench, Bartholomew Dillon. Kildare sought to block the appointment of Cromwell's preferred candidate, Christopher Delahide, by interceding with Wiltshire, his traditional ally at the English court. Other lesser appointments, such as those of Thomas Cusack and Thomas Finglas, were also delayed for several months because of Kildare's stubbornness and Cromwell's desire not to aggravate Kildare and therefore frustrate any future successful implementation of the envisaged reforms. Thus any hopes which the king's secretary might have entertained for immediate results from this policy were severely modified by his having to compete with influential Geraldine allies, notably Norfolk and Wiltshire, at court. The fact that Ossory backed Cromwell's reform resulted in Kildare's rejection of the king's secretary as an impartial arbitrator just as Wolsey had been during the 1520s. The evidence suggests that from the summer of 1533 onwards Cromwell was preparing the way for launching a full-scale programme for political reform in Ireland and that his plan for the Kildares was 'reform not damnation'.[11]

Cromwell's attempts at reconstructing the Dublin administration, however, bore little fruit.[12] Thus, while it is important not to exaggerate the impact of Cromwell's reformist endeavours, it is equally clear that Kildare was not indifferent to the implications of this trend for his retention of his position of authority should it continue. The royal reprimand incurred by the earl in August 1533 for his obstinacy in resisting the appointment of Cromwell's candidates testifies to his determination to resist any such efforts to whittle away his authority in the Dublin administration. It also provides proof of a hardening of the crown's attitude to the earl. Cromwell's initiatives were thus frustrating Kildare's exercise of control over the official medium for communication with the king. By mid-1533 the earl even appeared concerned regarding his ability to uphold appointments which he had already made. In endeavouring to superintend Kildare, Cromwell was only aggravating the earl all the more, yet failing to offset his influence.[13]

In the autumn and winter months of 1533 political pressure against Kildare was steadily mounting both in Dublin and at court. Soon after receiving a royal reprimand he transferred the king's ordnance to his own strongholds, chiefly to his castle at Maynooth, ostensibly to equip him to defend the Pale. In reality, however, this was a manoeuvre designed to enable him to cause disturbances in the Pale area in the event of his being removed from office. Developments in Ireland were now viewed with great suspicion by Henry, and so in September 1533 Kildare, Ossory and other officials of the Dublin government were summoned to the court. The summons had a twofold objective. Firstly, Henry and Cromwell sought to pacify the feud between the two earls and to secure a formal indenture from both, binding them to cooperate with Cromwell's efforts to resuscitate crown government, including its extension into their own territories.¹⁴ Cromwell was especially anxious to bring Kildare to court before launching his reform programme. He believed that in London the earl could be open to persuasion from high-ranking courtiers, inducing him to conform to these disagreeable reforms. In addition, his removal from Ireland would minimise his opportunities for fomenting trouble locally at the very delicate initial stages of introducing the reform programme. Moreover, it would provide the government with a hostage for the compliance of his kinsmen and supporters in the lordship.¹⁵

At the same time the Irish council sent over a major indictment of Anglo-Irish magnates in general, and of Kildare and Ossory in particular, claiming that disorder was widespread, that the two earls were locked in ongoing feuding, and that the colony itself was therefore rendered extremely vulnerable to attack. Even Kildare's own brother, Sir James Fitzgerald, complained that he was being oppressed by Gerald and that the earl was destroying Counties Kildare and Carlow by his imposition of excessive exactions on the local population. The councillors also made recommendations for administrative reform and advocated the appointment of an experienced English Lord Deputy.¹⁶ Cromwell's discussions with Henry regarding the dispute between the Earls of Kildare and Ossory evolved into a full-scale critique of Kildare's control and patronage. At court Robert Cowley, a close ally of the Butlers, pressed the attack against Kildare on Ossory's behalf.¹⁷

Nevertheless, the government's handling of Kildare necessitated patient diplomacy rather than precipitate action. Henry therefore reiterated his summons to Kildare to attend court, but tempered it with a gesture of reassurance and goodwill by granting the earl the right to nominate his own deputy upon his departure for London.¹⁸ Kildare, however, had ignored the king's warning against continuing to transfer the king's ordnance from Dublin Castle. Having received a second summons, Kildare was placed in a dilemma. Experience had taught him the dangers and costs involved in such a call. Equally, Kildare had no way of being sure as to what Henry VIII intended, and so he was reluctant to risk forfeiting the chance of a political victory through blatant disobedience.¹⁹ He sensed the imminent threat to his retention of the deputyship; and it was then that the possibility of rebellion entered the designs of the Geraldines, although at this stage it is likely only to have been viewed as a contingency which could hopefully be avoided.[20]

By late 1533, however, developments in Ireland were superseded by the crisis arising from Henry's divorce and his schism with the papacy, both of which necessitated extensive reforms in the political and ecclesiastical spheres in order to render the realm an independent, secure, unitary commonwealth. As a direct result, the earl's summons to London had stirred the interest of Charles V, who instructed his ambassador in London, Eustace Chapuys, to find out all he could about Kildare and his plans. Chapuys reported that the earl's continued refusal to respond to the royal summons to attend court sparked fears by early 1534 that he might be planning a rebellion.[21] In December 1533 Cromwell was determined that 'some trusty person be sent into Ireland to see that dominion established and also to draw and adhere to the king as many [of] . . . the great Irish rebels as is possible'.[22] By that stage Kildare's dismissal had already been decided upon, and the next few months were characterised by steps directed towards effecting a smooth transfer of authority to another deputy.[23]

Kildare procrastinated until Henry conceded a commission enabling him to nominate a deputy during his absence. He duly appointed his son, Thomas, Lord Offaly, to this position before departing for court. By March the earl had appeared at court, his infirmity disappointing Chapuys, who concluded that his potential usefulness to the Spaniards in whatever designs they might have had against England was now virtually nil. Gerald was, he wrote, 'sick both in body and brain by the shot of a harquebus, which he received a long time ago, there is no hope of his recovery'.[24] The view that Kildare had passed his prime is evident in Chapuys's switching his interest to Offaly, 'who, to judge from appearances, promises to be a valuable auxiliary in case of need, though still very young'.[25]

In early March Cromwell in a memorandum reminded himself 'to send my lord of Kildare the copy of the articles'. These articles are thought to have been intended to form the basis for a formal indenture regulating the relationship between Kildare and royal government in a similar manner to the indenture formally ratified by Henry VIII in the case of Ossory in late May.[26] This memorandum may well have been alluding to Cromwell's intention to open negotiations with Kildare with a view to concluding an agreement as he had done with Ossory, and there is no reason to believe that Kildare was being treated any differently from Ossory. This indenture proposed 'considerably more than the removal of Kildare from office, though substantially less than the destruction of the dynasty'.[27] He looked set to lose his ascendancy in central government. His local status was also to be redefined in an effort to eradicate elements of sovereignty which accrued to it. His hegemony at county level would be undermined by the reintroduction of the machinery of central administration.[28] His authority to exercise jurisdiction over neighbouring Gaelic septs or disobedient Anglo-Irish lords was also to be curtailed.

By the end of April the king was acutely sensitive to the possibly implications of Kildare's state of health. Realising that Gerald was 'not like to live long', he found Offaly's disposition in Ireland particularly worrying.[29] The death of Gerald would deprive the government of their hostage who was to be guarantor for introducing the Cromwellian reform programme, while at the same time leaving his son in the position of unrivalled leader of his dynasty and capable of sabotaging the reforms. In spite of his weakened state which impeded his examination, by May Kildare was deemed by the English council to have committed 'manifold enormities'. Consequently, he was dismissed from the deputyship and prevented from returning to Ireland, though not imprisoned. Events began rapidly to unfold. At the beginning of the month the earl dispatched three senior members of his retinue in London to Ireland in order to advise his son. These were followed a number of weeks later by some of the earl's most intimate circle, two of whom were members of his family. Henry then dispatched Thomas Cusack and Thomas Finglas to Offaly with a summons to attend court, as well as with instructions for the conduct of government during his absence. By then Kildare had attempted to pre-empt Henry's move by sending a message to his son cautioning him 'not to trust the king's council there' since they would advise him to obey the royal summons and travel to

England, where his life would be in danger. Offaly had also learned of a report by Thomas Canon, Skeffington's secretary, to the effect that he and all of his uncles would be captured, transferred to England and executed. Contrary to Stanihurst's version of events, Canon did not state that Gerald had been executed, but it was also rumoured that Cusack and others would receive rewards from the king for undertaking to capture Thomas and his five uncles. Such rumours, though unfounded, are a clear indication of the anxious and mistrustful attitude of the Geraldines at this point.[30]

With his father mortally ill, and his own replacement as deputy imminent, Offaly had no guarantee of his own personal safety or that of his family. He had received ominous warning from his father regarding his future should he comply with Henry's summons to attend court, and he had no real reason to suppose that co-operating with the king would ensure his dynasty's continued dominance of Irish political affairs. On the basis of his father's and grandfather's experience, Offaly reckoned that in mounting a show of Geraldine indispensability he could force Henry and Cromwell to reverse or postpone their plans for reform in such a way as to accommodate them to Geraldine dominance.[31]

By the end of May both Kildare and Offaly were aware that proceedings were afoot to reappoint Skeffington as Lord Deputy. On 30 May Ossory subscribed to an indenture by which he bound himself to act 'in all and every thing, as appertaineth to their duties of allegiance of an English subject'.[32] Thus, the final provisions for launching Cromwell's reforms were put in place during the month of May 1534. Skeffington was to replace Kildare as Lord Deputy and was to preside over a reshuffled administration. Patrick Finglas, a strong opponent of Kildare, was appointed Chief Justice of the King's Bench early that month. The *Ordinances for the Government of Ireland* were printed, and Ossory had agreed to be bound to their implementation. Cusack and Finglas had been dispatched with instructions for Offaly.

Then the entire plan went astray. While Ossory proved content to comply with Cromwell's reform programme on 30 May 1534 in order to ensure his political survival, the Kildares showed no such readiness to relinquish their powerful position. It was

Ossory's vulnerability which was to be his salvation. Ossory lacked allies at court since he was at odds with Norfolk and Wiltshire, and he did not have a certain title to the Ormond earldom. He therefore hoped to gain both by lending his support to Cromwell. By contrast, Kildare's strength, based on a secure title to the earldom, his local hegemony and influential court alliances, served to stiffen his resolve in resisting the reform programme's implementation and caused him to be swept aside as a result not of the policy itself but rather of his inflexible response to it.[33] Indeed, the Kildares had comparatively stronger grounds for adopting such a stance, since, unlike Ossory, whose liberty of Tipperary was allowed to remain untouched, Gerald's liberty of County Kildare was to be abolished under the new reform programme outlined in the *Ordinances for the Government of Ireland*. This threat to the earl's county liberty was undoubtedly the most sorely felt and essentially the only direct incursion made on Kildare's position at this point. But there were other more subtle yet offensive moves afoot to undermine the earl's position both in ecclesiastical affairs and as a landed magnate.

Concurrent with his problems in retaining his position in the political sphere, the ninth earl had encountered some difficulties in exercising his authority in the ecclesiastical affairs of Kildare during the 1520s. The earl claimed to have secured a promise from Henry VIII in 1515 that he might be allowed to nominate the successor to the then Bishop of Kildare, Edmund Lane. However, when Gerald sought to assert this privilege following Lane's death in 1523, the king did not concur with his choice of candidate and instead appointed Thomas Dillon to the see. Moreover, Dillon was appointed during Kildare's enforced absence at the English court in 1526. The earl did not contest Dillon's appointment, probably because he was too preoccupied with the difficult tasks of retaining his control over the Dublin government and regaining the deputyship, both of which undoubtedly ranked higher on his list of priorities than the appoinment of a candidate to the politically insignificant see of Kildare.[34] Nonetheless, while Kildare was by no means unique in having his recommendation ignored, the fact that this nomination 'right' concerned the see of Kildare, much of which fell within his liberty jurisdiction, surely aggrieved Gerald. Thereafter the earl also had a very fractious relationship with Bishop Dillon's successor, Walter Wellesley, who was also prior of one of the county's largest monastic houses, Connell Abbey. Given that he had succeeded to the bishopric during Kildare's absence, Wellesley needed to exercise caution in his dealings with Gerald. Yet, by virtue of his alliance with the Duke of Norfolk at court, Wellesley was able for the most part to operate independently of Kildare's control. The bishop was no supporter of Gerald: as early as February 1529 he made his position public by signing his name to a list of members of the Irish council who opposed the earl. Indeed, so intense was the animosity between the two that Wellesley claimed that Kildare had once threatened to kill him.[35] Such incidents, however, did not amount to a serious dissipation of the earl's position.

By far the most serious challenge to Kildare's authority which emerged from ecclesiastical quarters was that posed by Archbishop John Alen, who presided over the metropolitan see of Dublin during the period 1529–34. James Murray argues that Kildare himself recognised the gravity of the archbishop's designs for reclaiming archiepiscopal lands and that Alen's murder at the hands of Offaly's forces at Artane on 28 July 1534 stemmed from animosity dating from this time.[36] The revival of archiepiscopal rights and prerogatives had its beginnings during the episcopacies of Alen's predecessors, William Rokeby and Hugh Inge, although down to the late 1520s that policy had little real effect on Kildare's influence in ecclesiastical affairs and his occupation of see lands. However, Alen was implicated in the political machinations directed by Wolsey in 1529 which aimed to mitigate the dominance exerted by the overmighty ninth Earl of Kildare in Irish affairs. It was from that point onwards that the simultaneous yet separate processes of a gradual endeavour to curb the earl's political dominance on the one hand and resistance of his assertion of rights of ownership of archiepiscopal lands in south Dublin, south-east Kildare and Wicklow on the other became merged and intensified.

Alen's opposition to Kildare had begun in the political arena when, only a month after his arrival in Dublin, the archbishop conducted an investigation which provided evidence that Kildare was inciting his retainers to cause disturbances in the lordship.[37]

Murray suggests that Kildare had his revenge on Alen following Wolsey's fall, with the earl possibly playing a role in the factional intrigue at court which resulted in Alen's being served a crippling *praemunire* fine. Kildare definitely fended off Alen's claims to certain properties which the archbishop contested. He further avenged Alen's attempts to undermine his political authority and his standing as a landed magnate when, on his return to power in 1532, he procured the archbishop's removal from the chancellorship and replaced him with Alen's archiepiscopal rival, George Cromer, Archbishop of Armagh. Kildare thus proved he was still in a sufficiently strong position to be able to manipulate problematic primates as his father had done in order to isolate his opponents in the Dublin administration. For the time being Kildare appeared to have reduced the threat posed by Alen, although the archbishop's alliance with Cromwell ensured that he would remain a thorn in the side of the earl.

These concurrent challenges to Kildare's position added substantially to his sense of imminent threat in the years immediately preceding 1534. But the actual crisis of the Kildares was precipitated in the early summer of 1534 when Cromwell began proceedings to reappoint Skeffington as Lord Deputy. The choice of this official who was on bad terms with Kildare did much to limit the possibilities for Cromwell's reform programme, since it alienated the one figure on whom a great deal depended for its effective implementation, and before August 1534 there is no evidence of a new policy actually being implemented in the lordship. As a result of the regular exchange of intelligence between Kildare and his son, there was little chance of a successful outcome to Cusack's and Finglas's overtures to Offaly; and at his father's instigation, Offaly resolved to adopt a 'well-established, if dangerous, policy of resort to disorder and revolt'.[38] On St Barnabas's Day, 11 June 1534, he arrived at a meeting of the king's council in St Mary's Abbey, accompanied by up to 1,000 horsemen and foot-soldiers. In a gesture of protest, Offaly threw down the sword of state, resigned his office as governor's deputy, and renounced the king's policies. This and subsequent acts of defiance on Offaly's part were probably not conceived as shows of outright revolt, but rather as shows of Kildare indispensability, with the purpose of securing the dynasty's reinstatement to its position of dominance in the lordship. Yet it is difficult to see how Henry VIII could have regarded their behaviour as anything but rebellion. As Steven Ellis has stressed, Offaly's action came at a time when the king was openly defying both Charles V and the pope and when Cromwell was engaged in steering through parliament a whole battery of reforms which were designed to legitimate the break with Rome.[39] In response to his son's defiance, Kildare, who was regarded as being the principal architect of the rebellion, was imprisoned in the Tower on 29 June and was there detained until his death in September 1534. The revolt caught Henry and Cromwell by surprise, and it was not until August that the king became galvanised into action, resolving to dispatch Skeffington and a force of 2,300 men to crush the insurrection. Throughout the summer months Henry made promises of pardon, absolution for the Geraldine forces who had murdered Archbishop Alen and the release of Kildare in his effort to hasten an end to the revolt. In addition, official rumours circulated in the English court to the effect that Offaly was on the point of requesting the king's pardon, or that he had already surrendered. Offaly, however, made no such request, and his father was fully supportive of his rebellious stance. It was reported that 'Whenever people happen to mention the subject before him, the earl invariably praises his son's purpose, instead of blaming him, and shows great contentment at his present work, only wishing that he was older and more experienced in warfare.'[40] Kildare's old ally, the Duke of Norfolk, declared that Cromwell and Skeffington were to blame for having precipitated this revolt through their adoption of such a hostile attitude towards the earl.

While the final preparations were afoot for the dispatch of Skeffington's forces, Gerald, ninth Earl of Kildare, died in the Tower of London on 2 September 1534, his wife, Elizabeth having remained with him constantly throughout his imprisonment. The earl is said to have been buried in St Peter's Church in the Tower, and his wife took up residence in Beaumanoir in Leicestershire, the home of her brother, Lord Leonard Grey. She left her eldest son, Gerald, in Ireland, and he remained in the care of his aunt, Lady Eleanor MacCarthy, until he went into exile on the continent in 1540.

The earl's death provided a unique opportunity for Henry VIII. Should he succeed in defeating Thomas, now tenth Earl of Kildare, he could look forward to the complete elimination of this overmighty dynasty from the Irish polity. At the time of Gerald's death his son was facing into a conflict with the king's army which no Earl of Kildare had undertaken before.

The events of the Kildare rebellion itself belong to a different study and have already been dealt with in detail by Laurence McCorristine.[41] When the dust had settled after the suppression of the revolt in August 1535, it remained to address the question of the posthumous attainder of the ninth earl and that of his son and his supporters. While proving the treasonous offences committed by Earl Thomas and his supporters was straightforward, the provision of sound evidence of Earl Gerald's culpability of treason was a great deal more problematic for the English government. Given that the government's case was so weak, a long preamble was appended to his indictment, recording his alleged treasonous offences. He was declared to have committed treason through his association in 1524–5 with Desmond, who was engaged in intrigues with Francis I and Charles V. A second charge of treason rested on Kildare's incitement of attacks on Delvin and the king's subjects in 1528. Both offences were undoubtedly treasonous; the problem was, however, that Kildare had already been pardoned for these two offences. Consequently, the government's case against him relied on three allegations of misconduct in the period 1532–4. On the first count, Kildare was accused of having allowed O'Neill and Sir John Fitzgerald to invade County Louth while he himself raided County Kilkenny and robbed the king's subjects at Castledermot fair in 1532–3. Secondly, he was said to have blatantly disregarded the king's formal communication instructing him to desist from removing the royal artillery from Dublin Castle and from supplying ammunition to the Gaelic Irish. Thirdly, he was deemed culpable of treason for having appointed his son Thomas as his deputy and for advising him to heed the direction of the Irish council members who incited him to rebel against Henry VIII. However, Kildare's offences in 1532–3 were closer to being felonious than treasonous, and his removal of the king's ordnance in 1533–4 was not a treasonous offence. Nonetheless, Gerald was guilty of treason by virtue of having engineered the rebellion headed by his son. However, it is unlikely that the government could have presented sufficient evidence about his role in the rebellion in pursuing a treason conviction in common law. The real reason for Gerald's posthumous attainder was the government's decision that this was the most effective means of ensuring a clean-cut removal of the Fitzgerald family from their position of power.[42] The definitive act of attainder was eventually passed in May 1536.

The character of the administration of the lordship which subsequently emerged stood in stark contrast with that over which Gerald, ninth Earl of Kildare, and his father before him had presided for more than fifty years. As D. B. Quinn has stated, 'The course of English policy and interests in relation both to the outlying parts of England and Wales, and also to the international situation, was such that a new effort to integrate Ireland more fully into the dominions of the king was becoming increasingly probable.'[43] At government level, the impact of the removal of the Kildares was twofold. Firstly, with the annihilation of the only lord with sufficient power to govern the lordship on the king's behalf, Henry was compelled to adopt a policy which until now he had rejected: namely, the establishment of a permanent administration, manned by an English Lord Deputy backed by a standing army. Deprived of Kildare's interventionist presence in negotiating with Gaelic septs, the Dublin administration was now faced with an alien Gaelic society which was hostile towards the new English presence in the Dublin government with its English deputy and senior office-holders. Secondly, the attainder of the heads of the senior branches of the Fitzgerald family and of their allies yielded substantial tracts of land to the crown. These, combined with revenues and property from the dissolution of monastic and mendicant houses and land confiscated from absentee landlords in the name of the king, all provided Henry VIII with a firm financial footing on the short term at least on which he could build his position.

At local level, the crisis of the early 1530s wreaked havoc throughout County Kildare, causing serious distress to the local population, and the sudden removal of the Fitzgeralds left immediate, tangible after-effects. In August 1535 Kildare was described as having six of its eight baronies 'all burnt; few or no people inhabiting there, but leaving their corn in the ground to the traitors'.[44] Two years after the suppression of the revolt Lord Deputy Grey still remarked the county's devastated condition, reporting that

> The inhabitants of the county of Kildare . . . were most principal offenders in this rebellion, whereby they be in such fear (especially now since the execution of the Geraldines) as they dare not trust to abide in the country, but wandering about.[45]

Following the quelling of the rebellion, and with the Fitzgeralds removed from their position of supremacy, the liberty of Kildare, as stipulated in the *Ordinances for the Government of Ireland*, was suppressed and the Dublin government once again gained access to the administration and defence of the shire which had become a virtual enclave of Kildare hegemony in the preceding decades. In ecclesiastical circles too, the collapse of the Kildare regime left a vacuum, since the earl had enjoyed the right to nominate candidates for twenty-three benefices before the rebellion in 1534.

Not all senior members of the cadet branches of the Fitzgerald family had supported Offaly's rebellious stance: Sir James, Walter and Richard Fitzgerald, all uncles of Thomas, opposed the rebellion but were nonetheless captured at a banquet in Kilmainham. Offaly's other uncles, Oliver and John, were also apprehended, even before they heard news of their nephew's capture. All five were executed, along with Thomas, at Tyburn in February 1537. Apart from these individuals, only a handful of the extended Fitzgerald family were in fact implicated in or directly affected by the revolt. Thus, in spite of the virtual annihilation of their principal branch of Maynooth, the confiscation of the Kildares' manors and lands and their exclusion from receiving dissolved monastic properties, the extended comital Fitzgerald family remained by far the most influential landed family in sixteenth-century Kildare gentry society, retaining possession of their vast estates which extended across the whole of central Kildare, as well as the north-east and west of the county.

CONCLUSION

The deconstruction of Richard Stanihurst's romanticised tale of the fall of the house of Kildare has been a slow process. In the historiography of the past twenty-five years in particular, Gerald Fitzgerald, ninth Earl of Kildare, has gradually been stripped of the apologetic veneer in which Stanihurst enveloped him in order that he be exonerated from blame for the offence caused to the monarchy and the ensuing destruction of his household which still loomed so large in contemporary consciousness. Exposed to the assessment of late twentieth-century historians, a different appreciation of Gerald and of the complex political sphere within which he operated has emerged. In the process the earl has attracted some criticism for his lack of political judgement and personal charisma.

Increasingly, however, a more nuanced picture is emerging of a cautious, calculating, politically astute magnate who balanced efforts to assert his control over Gaelic septs with trying to maintain a strong cohort of support in the Irish council. He was obliged to contend with Cardinal Wolsey, who is reputed to have hated his guts, and then later with the wily Thomas Cromwell. He constantly fought to regain the deputyship when ousted from that coveted position, and he was ever mindful of the debilitating effect which his ongoing feud with the Butlers had on his power in the lordship. Most importantly of all, Kildare was faced with the challenge of the Cromwellian reform programme whose implementation was openly on the cards in the early months of 1534.

It is important not to regard the earl as steadily and irrevocably losing his power as a result of the encroachments of both secular and ecclesiastical agencies to a point where he was put in a defensive position in the early 1530s. In 1532 Kildare had won his fight to regain the deputyship and had set about working out his strategy for dealing with the Dublin council and Cromwell. To argue that the last years of Kildare rule were marked by signs of an inevitable slide towards rebellion is to allow the hindrance of hindsight to colour our understanding of the nature of the relationship between Cromwell's regime and the earl. It is, moreover, an indictment of Gerald's political capabilities, underestimating as it does his obvious sensitivity to the changes occurring around him. It also ignores Cromwell's efforts to cajole Kildare into accepting his reform programme and the sensitivity with which both he and Henry VIII endeavoured to handle the earl in the early months of 1534.

The difficulties facing the Earl of Kildare in May 1534 were by no means insurmountable, but his arrogance in inciting his son to make a show of Geraldine strength in the following month came at a time when both the king and his secretary were already known to be very anxious regarding the role of the Kildares as possible obstacles to the successful implementation of their reform programme. Against this backdrop of heightened tensions, the stakes were raised to crisis point with the outbreak of Offaly's rebellion. While Kildare's misjudgement in his response to the reforms has long been acknowledged, it is only now that his achievement in wrestling to maintain his position within a rapidly evolving Tudor administration is coming to light, having been long since overshadowed by the calamitous destruction of his family and their political ascendancy in the mid-1530s.

NOTES

Introduction

[1] Richard Stanihurst, *The First Volume of the Chronicles of England, Scotland and Ireland by Raphael Holinshed* (London, 1577), p. 105.

[2] D. B. Quinn, 'The Hegemony of the Earls of Kildare, 1494–1520' in Art Cosgrove (ed.), *A New History of Ireland*, ii: *Medieval Ireland, 1169–1534* (Oxford, 1987; 1993 ed.), pp 656–7.

[3] R. Dudley Edwards, *Ireland under the Tudors* (Dublin, 1977), p. 39.

[4] S. G. Ellis, 'Tudor Policy and the Kildare Ascendancy in the Lordship of Ireland, 1496–1534', *Irish Historical Studies*, xx, 79 (Mar. 1977), p. 250.

[5] S. G. Ellis, *Tudor Ireland: Crown, Community and the Conflict of Cultures, 1470–1603* (London, 1985), p. 101.

[6] See S. G. Ellis, *Tudor Frontiers and Noble Power: The Making of the British State* (Oxford, 1995).

1

[1] *Annála Connacht . . . 1224–1544*, ed. A. Martin Freeman (Dublin, 1944) (hereafter cited as *Ann. Conn.*), p. 623.

[2] Quinn, 'Hegemony of the Earls of Kildare', p. 656.

[3] Donough Bryan, *Gerald Fitzgerald, the Great Earl of Kildare, 1456–1513* (Dublin, 1933), p. 91.

[4] C. W. Fitzgerald, *The Earls of Kildare, 1157–1773* (Dublin, 1858), p. 27; Jocelyn Otway-Ruthven, 'The Medieval County of Kildare', *Irish Historical Studies*, xi, 43 (Mar. 1959), p. 181.

[5] Ellis, *Tudor Frontiers and Noble Power*, p. 112.

[6] Quinn, 'Hegemony of the Earls of Kildare', pp 648–9.

[7] Ellis, *Tudor Ireland*, pp 56–7; see also D. B. Quinn, ' "Irish" and "English" Ireland' in *New History of Ireland*, ii, 637.

[8] Colm Lennon, *Sixteenth-Century Ireland: The Incomplete Conquest* (Dublin, 1994), p. 71.

[9] Ellis, *Tudor Ireland*, p. 66.

[10] S. G. Ellis, *Reform and Revival: English Government in Ireland, 1470–1534* (Woodbridge, 1996), p. 60.

[11] Quinn, ' "Irish" and "English" Ireland', p. 636.

[12] For the strength and composition of Kildare's forces see Quinn, 'Hegemony of the Earls of Kildare', p. 652; Ellis, *Reform and Revival*, pp 50–54; Lennon, *Sixteenth-Century Ireland*, p. 72.

[13] Lennon, *Sixteenth-Century Ireland*, p. 74.

[14] Ellis, *Reform and Revival*, p. 56.

[15] Quinn, 'Hegemony of the Earls of Kildare', pp 651–2.

[16] For examples of tributes see *Crown Surveys of Lands, 1540–41, with the Kildare Rental begun in 1518*, ed. Gearóid MacNiocaill (Dublin, 1992); Lennon, *Sixteenth-Century Ireland*, p. 74.

[17] *Crown Surveys of Lands*, ed. MacNiocaill, pp 235–6.

[18] Ellis, *Tudor Ireland*, p. 92.

[19] Lennon, *Sixteenth-Century Ireland*, p. 52.
[20] *Crown Surveys of Lands*, ed. MacNiocaill, pp 266, 271.
[21] S. G. Ellis, 'The Destruction of the Liberties: Some Further Evidence', *Bull. Inst. Hist. Research*, liv (1981), p. 157; idem, *Reform and Revival*, p. 194.
[22] See H. F. Hore and James Graves (eds), *The Social State of the Southern and Eastern Counties of Ireland in the Sixteenth Century* (Dublin, 1870).
[23] *Crown Surveys of Lands*, ed. MacNiocaill, p. 356.
[24] Mary Ann Lyons, 'Church and Society in Early Sixteenth-Century Kildare' (M.A. thesis, St Patrick's College, Maynooth, 1991), pp 13–14.
[25] *Crown Surveys of Lands*, ed. MacNiocaill, p. 272.
[26] Lyons, 'Church and Society', p. 16.
[27] Ellis, *Tudor Ireland*, pp 93–4.
[28] Quinn, ' "Irish" Ireland and "English" Ireland', p. 623.
[29] Quinn, 'Hegemony of the Earls of Kildare', p. 656.
[30] Fitzgerald, *Earls of Kildare*, p. 82; Ellis, *Tudor Ireland*, pp 98, 332.
[31] Fitzgerald, *Earls of Kildare*, p. 63.

2

[1] Ellis, *Tudor Frontiers and Noble Power*, pp 127–8.
[2] Fitzgerald, *Earls of Kildare*, p. 119; *Crown Surveys of Lands*, ed. MacNiocaill, pp 319–51.
[3] *Crown Surveys of Lands*, ed. MacNiocaill, p. 314.
[4] Lennon, *Sixteenth-Century Ireland*, p. 83.
[5] Fitzgerald, *Earls of Kildare*, p. 108.
[6] Ibid., p. 120.
[7] Ellis, *Tudor Frontiers and Noble Power*, pp 131–2.
[8] Duke of Leinster (ed.), 'The Kildare Rental Book' in Historical Manuscripts Commission, *Ninth Report, Part II, Appendix* (London, 1884), p. 273.
[9] Ellis, 'Destruction of the Liberties', pp 155–7.
[10] Lennon, *Sixteenth-Century Ireland*, p. 71.
[11] See Mary Ann Lyons, 'Sidelights on the Kildare Ascendancy: A Survey of Geraldine Involvement in the Church, c. 1470 – c. 1520', *Archivium Hibernicum*, xlviii (1994), pp 73–87.
[12] Quoted in Fitzgerald, *Earls of Kildare*, p. 120.
[13] Mary Ann Lyons, 'The Foundation of the Geraldine College of the Blessed Virgin Mary, Maynooth, 1518', *Journal of the County Kildare Archaeological Society*, xviii, 2 (1994–5), pp 134–50.
[14] *Annála Ríoghachta Éireann: Annals of the Kingdom of Ireland by the Four Masters*, ed. John O'Donovan (7 vols, Dublin, 1851) (hereafter cited as *A.F.M.*), iii, 1327; *Ann. Conn.*, p. 631.
[15] Ellis, *Tudor Ireland*, pp 85, 94.
[16] Ibid., p. 92.
[17] *Ann. Conn.*, p. 625; *A.F.M.*, iii, 1329.
[18] *Ann .Conn.*, p. 627.
[19] Ibid., p. 631; *A.F.M.*, iii, 1337.
[20] *A.F.M.*, iii, 1341.
[21] Ibid., pp 1367, 1369, 1405, 1409–11, 1417; *Ann. Conn.*, pp 651, 661.
[22] Ellis, *Tudor Ireland*, p. 102.

[23] Lennon, *Sixteenth-Century Ireland*, p. 79.
[24] Ellis, *Tudor Ireland*, p. 103; idem, *Reform and Revival*, p. 185; idem, 'Destruction of the Liberties'.
[25] Quinn, 'Hegemony of the Earls of Kildare', p. 659; Lennon, *Sixteenth-Century Ireland*, p. 82; Lyons, 'Foundation of the Geraldine College'.
[26] Quinn, 'Hegemony of the Earls of Kildare', p. 658.
[27] Lennon, *Sixteenth-Century Ireland*, p. 79.
[28] Ellis, *Tudor Ireland*, p. 102.
[29] Ibid., pp 103–4.
[30] Quinn, 'Hegemony of the Earls of Kildare', pp 659–60.

3

[1] Ellis, *Tudor Ireland*, p. 105.
[2] Fitzgerald, *Earls of Kildare*, p. 85.
[3] Henry VIII to the Lord Lieutenant and council of Ireland [1520] (*S.P. Hen.VIII*, ii, pt iii, pp 33–4).
[4] Confession of Donogh O'Carroll [1520] (ibid., p. 45).
[5] Ellis, *Tudor Ireland*, p. 114.
[6] Ibid., p. 102.
[7] D. B. Quinn, 'The Reemergence of English Policy as a Major Factor in Irish Affairs, 1520–34' in *New History of Ireland*, ii, 668.
[8] Ibid., p. 670.
[9] Ibid.; Lennon, *Sixteenth-Century Ireland*, p. 95.
[10] Lennon, *Sixteenth-Century Ireland*, p. 95; Ellis, *Tudor Ireland*, p. 116.
[11] Ellis, *Tudor Ireland*, pp 116–17.
[12] Quinn, 'Reemergence of English Policy', p. 672.
[13] Lennon, *Sixteenth-Century Ireland*, p. 97.
[14] Quinn, 'Reemergence of English Policy', p. 672.
[15] Ibid.
[16] Ibid., p. 669.
[17] Ellis, *Tudor Ireland*, p. 117.
[18] Kildare to Henry VIII, 17 Aug. 1525 (*S.P. Hen.VIII*, ii, pt iii, p. 125).
[19] Fitzgerald, *Earls of Kildare*, p. 101; Ellis, *Tudor Ireland*, p. 117.
[20] Quinn, 'Reemergence of English Policy', p. 673.
[21] Ellis, *Tudor Ireland*, p. 117.
[22] See Fitzgerald, *Earls of Kildare*, pp 103–5.
[23] Lennon, *Sixteenth-Century Ireland*, pp 99–100.
[24] Ellis, *Tudor Ireland*, p. 118; Quinn, 'Reemergence of English Policy', p. 674.
[25] James Butler to Ormond, 27 Dec. 1527 (*L. & P., Hen.VIII*, iv, pt ii, no. 3698); Ellis, *Tudor Ireland*, p. 118.
[26] Archbishop Inge and Lord Chief Justice Bermingham to Wolsey, 23 Feb. 1528 (*S.P. Hen.VIII*, ii, pt iii, pp 126–8).
[27] Lennon, *Sixteenth-Century Ireland*, p. 98.
[28] Ellis, *Tudor Ireland*, p. 118.
[29] Quinn, 'Reemergence of English Policy', p. 675.
[30] Sir John Russell and Hennege to Wolsey, 28 July 1528 (*S.P. Hen.VIII*, ii, pt iii, p. 140n.); Ellis, *Tudor Ireland*, p. 119.

[31] Fitzgerald, *Earls of Kildare*, p. 107.
[32] Ibid.
[33] 'Instructions to be Shown unto the King's Highness' [1528] (*S.P. Hen.VIII*, ii, pt iii, p. 145).
[34] Ellis, *Tudor Ireland*, p. 119; Quinn, 'Reemergence of English Policy', p. 678; Lennon, *Sixteenth-Century Ireland*, p. 101.
[35] Quinn, 'Reemergence of English Policy', p. 678.
[36] Ibid., p. 679.
[37] Ibid.
[38] Fitzgerald, *Earls of Kildare*, p. 109.
[39] Ellis, *Tudor Ireland*, p. 120; Lennon, *Sixteenth-Century Ireland*, p. 102.
[40] Quinn, 'Reemergence of English Policy', p. 680; Lennon, *Sixteenth-Century Ireland*, p. 103.
[41] Quinn, 'Reemergence of English Policy', pp 680–81.
[42] Instructions to Thomas Cromwell [1532] (*S.P. Hen.VIII*, ii, pt iii, p. 156).
[43] Ellis, *Tudor Ireland*, p. 120; Quinn, 'Reemergence of English Policy', p. 681; Lennon, *Sixteenth-Century Ireland*, p. 103.
[44] Quoted in Lennon, *Sixteenth-Century Ireland*, p. 103.

4

[1] Ellis, 'Tudor Policy', p. 245.
[2] Ibid., p. 248.
[3] Ibid., p. 249.
[4] Quinn, 'The Reemergence of English Policy', p. 683.
[5] Ibid.
[6] Report to Cromwell [1533] (*S.P. Hen.VIII*, ii, pt iii, p. 169).
[7] Ibid.
[8] Laurence McCorristine, *The Revolt of Silken Thomas: A Challenge to Henry VIII* (Dublin, 1987), p. 46.
[9] Lennon, *Sixteenth-Century Ireland*, pp 103–4.
[10] Brendan Bradshaw, 'Cromwellian Reform and the Origins of the Kildare Rebellion, 1533–34', *Transactions of the Royal Historical Society*, 5th ser., xxvii (1977), p. 85.
[11] Ibid., p. 80.
[12] S. G. Ellis, 'Thomas Cromwell and Ireland, 1532–40', *Historical Journal*, xxiii (1980), p. 500.
[13] Ellis, 'Tudor Policy', p. 253.
[14] Bradshaw, 'Cromwellian Reform', p. 82.
[15] Ibid., p. 80.
[16] Ibid., p. 82.
[17] Ibid., p. 81.
[18] Ibid., p. 80.
[19] Ibid., pp 80–81.
[20] Ibid., p. 81.
[21] Chapuys to Charles V, 17 Jan. 1534 (*L. & P. Hen.VIII*, vii, no. 83); same to same, 29 Jan. 1534 (ibid., no. 121).
[22] The king's council [memorandum], Dec. 1533 (ibid., vi, no. 1487).

[23] Ellis, 'Tudor Policy', p. 255.
[24] Chapuys to Charles V, 22 Apr. 1534 (*L. & P. Hen.VIII*, vii, no. 530).
[25] Chapuys to High Commander of Leon, 22 Apr. 1534 (*Cal. S.P. Spain*, v, no. 45).
[26] Bradshaw, 'Cromwellian Reform', pp 83–4.
[27] Ibid., p. 87.
[28] Ibid.
[29] Gerald was, in fact, well enough to sign warrants on 30 April 1534: see Ellis, 'Tudor Policy', p. 257 n. 73.
[30] Bradshaw, 'Cromwellian Reform', pp 88–9.
[31] McCorristine, *Revolt of Silken Thomas*, p. 65.
[32] Ordinances for the Government of Ireland, 1534 (*S.P. Hen.VIII*, ii, pt iii, p. 207).
[33] Bradshaw, 'Cromwellian Reform', pp 87–8.
[34] Lyons, 'Church and Society', p. 100.
[35] Walter Wellesley, Bishop of Kildare, to Duke of Norfolk, 15 May 1539 (*Cal. Carew MSS, 1515–74*, p. 151; *L. & P. Hen. VIII*, xiv, pt i, no. 970); Augustine Valkenburg, 'Walter Wellesley, Bishop of Kildare, 147--1539' in *Journal of the County Kildare Archaeological Society*, xiv, 3 (1968), p. 538; Lyons, 'Sidelights on the Kildare Ascendancy', p. 79.
[36] P.R.O., SP 60/2/25; James Murray, 'Archbishop Alen, Tudor Reform and the Kildare Rebellion', *Proceedings of the Royal Irish Academy*, lxxxix, sect. C (1989), p. 1; Lyons, 'Church and Society', p. 107.
[37] P.R.O., SP 60/1/67; Ellis, *Tudor Ireland*, p. 119; Murray, 'Archbishop Alen', p. 14.
[38] McCorristine, *Revolt of Silken Thomas*, p. 65.
[39] Ellis, *Tudor Ireland*, p. 124.
[40] Chapuys to Charles V, 29 Aug. 1534 (*Cal. S.P. Spain*, v, no. 86); same to same, 10 Sept. 1534 (ibid., no. 87).
[41] See McCorristine, *Revolt of Silken Thomas*.
[42] S. G. Ellis, 'Henry VIII, Rebellion and the Rule of Law', *Historical Journal*, xxiv (1981), pp 521–2.
[43] Quinn, 'Reemergence of English Policy', p. 687.
[44] Gerald Aylmer and John Alen to Cromwell, 21 Aug. 1535 (*S.P. Hen. VIII*, ii, pt iii, p. 263); Lyons, 'Church and Society', p. 120.
[45] Grey and council to Henry VIII, 20 Apr. 1537 (*S.P. Hen.VIII*, ii, pt iii, pp 429–30); Lyons, 'Church and Society', p. 121.

SELECT BIBLIOGRAPHY

Among the principal primary sources for Gerald Fitzgerald's life and career is Richard Stanihurst's *The First Volume of the Chronicles of England, Scotland and Ireland by Raphael Holinshed* (London, 1577). Stanihurst provides colourful details of the earl's personality, but his portrayal of Kildare's political career is apologetic in favour of Gerald. The *State Papers, Henry VIII* (11 vols, London, 1830–52), the *Letters and Papers, Foreign and Domestic, Henry VIII* (21 vols, London, 1862–1932) and *Calendar of the Carew Manuscripts preserved in the Archiepiscopal Library at Lambeth* (6 vols, London, 1867–73) are all indispensable sources for the study of his political career. Important counterbalancing perspectives on Kildare are provided in the *Annála Connacht: The Annals of Connacht, A.D. 1224–1544*, ed. A. M. Freeman (Dublin, 1970) and in *Annála Ríoghachta Éireann: Annals of the Kingdom of Ireland by the Four Masters*, ed. John O'Donovan (7 vols, Dublin, 1851). On a more local level, 'The Kildare Rental Book', edited by the Duke of Leinster, in Historical Manuscripts Commission, *Ninth Report, Part II, Appendix* (London, 1884) has been largely superseded by the more recently published *Crown Surveys of Lands, 1540–41, with the Kildare Rental begun in 1518*, ed. Gearóid MacNiocaill (Dublin, 1992), but both provide a valuable insight into the mechanics of the operation of the Kildare estate and into the workings of the 'slantyaght' system.

For biographical information, there is a useful but uncritical and dated account of Gerald's life in C. W. Fitzgerald, *The Earls of Kildare, 1157–1773* (Dublin, 1858). Donough Bryan's *Gerald Fitzgerald, the Great Earl of Kildare, 1456–1513* (Dublin, 1933) is useful, though also very dated. Richard Bagwell, in his *Ireland under the Tudors* (3 vols, repr., London, 1962), posited a very traditional interpretation of the ninth earl's career which remained largely intact down to the 1970s; it is evident also in Brian Fitzgerald's *The Geraldines: An Experiment in Irish Government, 1169–1601* (London, 1951). That interpretation viewed Gerald as less capable politically than his father had been; blame for the outbreak of the Geraldine rebellion was generally attributed to Lord Offaly, and Kildare was deemed innocent of any involvement with the planning of the revolt. However, Brendan Bradshaw's article 'Cromwellian Reform and the Origins of the Kildare Rebellion, 1533–34', *Transactions of the Royal Historical Society*, 5th ser., xxvii (1977) was one of several works which jettisoned that traditional interpretation and subjected the study of the last years of Gerald's political career to more rigorous scrutiny within the broader context of Anglo-Irish relations in the early 1530s. D. B. Quinn's four chapters, 'The Hegemony of the Earls of Kildare, 1494–1520', 'Tudor Policy and the Kildare Ascendancy in the Lordship of Ireland, 1496–1534', 'The Reemergence of English Policy as a Major Factor in Irish Affairs, 1520–34' and ' "Irish" Ireland and "English" Ireland', published in Art Cosgrove (ed.), *A New History of Ireland*, ii: *Medieval Ireland, 1169–1534* (Oxford, 1993 ed.), have served to modernise scholarly opinion on the Kildare ascendancy, though Quinn viewed the ninth earl as less capable in the field of politics than his father had been.

By far the greatest contribution to the study of the Kildare dynasty's involvement in national politics has been that of Steven Ellis. His *Tudor Ireland: Crown, Community and the Conflict of Cultures, 1470–1603* (London, 1985) and *Reform and Revival: English Government in Ireland, 1470–1534* (Woodbridge, 1986) both bring to light a wholly fresh perspective on the practical workings of the Kildare ascendancy. His comparative work, *Tudor Frontiers and Noble Power: The Making of the British State* (Oxford, 1995), has provided a more balanced, contextualised assessment of the ascendancy of the Kildares by viewing them not in isolation but rather as one of several powerful dynasties involved in government within the framework of the wider Tudor state. Furthermore, his series of articles including 'Tudor Policy and the Kildare Ascendancy in the Lordship of Ireland, 1496–1534', *Irish Historical Studies*, xx, no. 79 (Mar. 1977), 'Thomas Cromwell and Ireland, 1532–40', *Historical Journal*, xxiii (1980), 'The Destruction of the Liberties: Some Further Evidence', *Institute of Historical Research Bulletin*, liv (1981) and 'Henry VIII, Rebellion and the Rule of Law', *Historical Journal*, xxiv (1981) have served to identify and tease out some of the complexities of the circumstances surrounding the demise of the Geraldines. Ellis's work has been complemented by Laurence McCorristine's reappraisal of the Kildare rebellion in 1534 in his work *The Revolt of Silken Thomas: A Challenge to Henry VIII* (Dublin, 1987), and the result has been the dismantling of the simplified, romantic interpretation of the fall of the Kildares posited by Stanihurst.

Recent work by James Murray, Steven Ellis and Mary Ann Lyons has investigated the role of the Kildares in church affairs. Murray's 'Archbishop Alen, Tudor Reform and the Kildare Rebellion', *Proceedings of the Royal Irish Academy*, lxxxix, sect. C (1989) examines the animosity between the eighth and ninth earls on the one hand, and Archbishop Alen on the other, concerning possession of archiepiscopal lands. Ellis, in his article 'The Kildare Rebellion and the Early Henrician Reformation', *Historical Journal*, xix, 4 (1976), investigates the significance of the Geraldine revolt with regard to the adoption of the Reformation in Ireland and also assesses the religious dimension to the rebellion. Lyons's 'Sidelights on the Kildare Ascendancy: A Survey of Geraldine Involvement in the Church, *c.* 1470 – *c.* 1520', *Archivium Hibernicum*, xlviii (1994), her 'The Foundation of the Geraldine College of the Blessed Virgin Mary, Maynooth, 1518', *Journal of the County Kildare Archaeological Society*, xviii, 2 (1994–5) and her unpublished M.A. thesis 'Church and Society in Sixteenth-Century Kildare' (St Patrick's College, Maynooth, 1991) explore the involvement of the Earls of Kildare in church patronage and clerical appointments, as well as assessing the impact of their demise in ecclesiastical affairs. Colm Lennon, *Sixteenth-Century Ireland: The Incomplete Conquest* (Dublin, 1994) and M. E. Collins, *Ireland, 1478–1610* (Dublin, 1980) both provide very useful surveys of this period.

HISTORICAL ASSOCIATION OF IRELAND
Life and Times Series

●

'The Historical Association of Ireland is to be congratulated for its **Life and Times** Series of biographies. They are written in an authoritative, accessible and enjoyable way'
History Ireland

'Invaluable *Life and Times* series'
Irish Times

'Students, tutors and the reading public will appreciate these short snapshots of key personalities'
Irish Historical Studies

'An excellent series'
John A. Murphy, *Sunday Independent*

●

No. 1 — HENRY GRATTAN
by JAMES KELLY

'The series has set a rigorous standard with this short study'
Books Ireland

'A succinct and thoughtful account of Grattan's career'
Eighteenth-Century Ireland

No. 2 — SIR EDWARD CARSON
by ALVIN JACKSON

'A scintillating essay in reappraisal'
K. Theodore Hoppen, *Irish Historical Studies*

'Jackson's splendid *Sir Edward Carson*'
Irish Times

No. 3 — EAMON DE VALERA
by PAURIC TRAVERS

'A good short summary of a very long political life'

Stair

No. 4 — D. P. MORAN
by PATRICK MAUME

'Written with a fine sense of detachment and objectivity'

Leader

No. 5 — HANNA SHEEHY SKEFFINGTON
by MARIA LUDDY

'Recommended without reservation'

Books Ireland

No. 6 — SHANE O'NEILL
by CIARAN BRADY

'A richly documented analysis'
John A. Murphy, Sunday Independent

'An exciting book. A little masterpiece'
Denis Faul, Seanchas Ard Mhacha

No. 7 — JUSTIN McCARTHY
by EUGENE J. DOYLE

'Successfully confutes F. S. L. Lyons's picture of McCarthy as a weak and vacillating successor to Parnell'

Irish Historical Studies